Advance Praise for
Let Your Heartbreak Be Your Guide

"Adam Bucko has been shaped by many rich, diverse streams of faith and is able to spit out the bones when it comes to the stuff that can choke you. He is deeply rooted in Jesus, and like Jesus, defies labels and categories. One of my basic prayers has been that what makes God cry would make me cry and what makes God laugh would make me laugh, and that is the prayer at the heart of this wonderful book."

—**Shane Claiborne**, author, *Irresistable Revolution*
co-founder, Red Letter Christians

"Father Adam Bucko represents the best of the Christian tradition. *Let Your Heartbreak Be Your Guide* is incarnational. He writes with the heart of Thomas Merton and soul of Dorothy Day."

—**Rev. Osagyefo Uhuru Sekou**
activist, musician, pastor; author, *urbansouls*

"Adam Bucko operates from both the heart and the head and is honest about his and our brokenness and limits. Above all, he invites all to become the spiritual workers and servants we are called to be in these times of darkness and hope on the cusp of becoming a new-born humanity."

—**Matthew Fox,** author, *Original Blessing*
and *The Coming of the Cosmic Christ*

Let Your Heartbreak Be Your Guide

Let Your Heartbreak Be Your Guide

Lessons in Engaged Contemplation

ADAM BUCKO

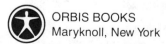

ORBIS BOOKS
Maryknoll, New York

Second Printing, February 2023

Founded in 1970, Orbis Books endeavors to publish works that enlighten the mind, nourish the spirit, and challenge the conscience. The publishing arm of the Maryknoll Fathers and Brothers, Orbis seeks to explore the global dimensions of the Christian faith and mission, to invite dialogue with diverse cultures and religious traditions, and to serve the cause of reconciliation and peace. The books published reflect the views of their authors and do not represent the official position of the Maryknoll Society. To learn more about Orbis Books, please visit our website at www.orbisbooks.com.

Manufactured in the United States of America

Library of Congress Cataloging-in-Publication Data

Names: Bucko, Adam, 1975- author.
Title: Let your heartbreak be your guide : lessons in engaged
    contemplation / Adam Bucko.
Description: Maryknoll, New York : Orbis Books, [2022] | Summary:
    "Reflections and intentional spiritual practices for the growing
    number of people living at the intersection of contemplation and
    justice" — Provided by publisher.
Identifiers: LCCN 2022003421 (print) | LCCN 2022003422 (ebook) |
    ISBN 9781626984769 (trade paperback) | ISBN 9781608339389
    (epub)
Subjects: LCSH: Contemplation. | Spiritual life—Catholic Church.
Classification: LCC BV5091.C7 B83 2022 (print) | LCC BV5091.C7
    (ebook) | DDC 248.3/4—dc23/eng/20220601
LC record available at https://lccn.loc.gov/2022003421
LC ebook record available at https://lccn.loc.gov/2022003422

This book is dedicated to my mentors and teachers:

Halina and Richard Bucko,
Matthew Fox, Andrew Harvey,
Rabbi Yehuda Fine, Marcellus Bear Heart William,
Tessa Bielecki, Sr. Vandana Mataji,
Swami Satchidananda, Shree Anandi Ma,
Dr. Rod Bush, Sr. Michaela and Br. Francis,
Fr. Thomas Keating, Rev. Leng Lim, Taslim Tagore,
and all of our kids at The Reciprocity Foundation

Contents

Lost and Found

A few years ago, in the days leading up to my ordination as a priest, I was trying to make sense of the journey I had taken to get there. As I re-examined how God had generously led me, my mind and heart reached back to a community where I had once lived. The community was an ecumenical Christian community—a quasi-monastic community, if you will—located in the slums of India, where prayer and works of mercy met beautifully in sacred service offered to victims of AIDS, abuse, homelessness, and social estrangement.

As I re-experience that environment, I see clearly all the people who were brought to us every day. I see their broken souls. I see their gangrene-infected bodies, filled with maggots. I still smell their wounds. I feel their very visible pain.

But I also hear the bell calling everyone to chapel for morning prayers, and then I see the procession of broken and deformed bodies moving slowly toward the place of worship. Some are walking, some crawling; and because some are missing limbs, some are limping. All of them are moving slowly toward prayer, understanding that what is about to take place will somehow infuse them with new life. Making their pain visible to God and their brothers and sisters and siblings will strengthen them and make them better.

I also see the Missionaries of Charity, all those sisters of Mother Teresa's, who liked visiting us sometimes. They would arrive after a two-hour drive, spent silently praying the rosary, and make their way into our community, entering it gently, always starting with the tuberculosis ward, filled with patients who struggled with multi-drug-resistant TB. It felt like each time they would find just the right person, the sickest and the weakest person, approach them gently, touch their feet as a sign of reverence, and then care for them in a way that, even today, moves me to tears. In their minds they were meeting Christ, and the pain they were witnessing was the pain of their savior who was being crucified in front of them. That pain was to be met, embraced, and cared for.

So when I reflect on my calling today, and on how I hope one day to have the guts and fortitude and courage to say yes to God, I am reminded of that place where I witnessed people whose complete yes to God created a container of grace where people were able to come in and be reassembled. Time and time again, brokenness was turned into wholeness, chaos into clarity and purpose, and the lost were finally found. God really lived there with us in that little community of broken people.

I desperately want this same Engaged Contemplation to fill my life today, in my work as a priest and in my role as a member of the human family in the place where I make home. Each of the reflections in this book are born from this deep desire for devotion and faithfulness, and for companions who are broken like me, like all of us, in one way or another.

Are you familiar with the following two parables in the Gospel that are so full of rich images that speak of our human predicament and our tendency to get lost?

In the first—the Parable of the Lost Sheep—we are presented with an image of a sheep that leaves the fold and wanders off on its own. Early Christians did not hesitate to view the lost sheep as a metaphor for what happens in our own lives. We become distracted; we move quickly or thoughtlessly from one thing to another, but then there are glimpses of God that we see along the way.

In the second—the Parable of the Lost Coin—the image we are given is that of a woman with a lamp who refuses to give up and tirelessly searches for a lost coin. Again, early Christians didn't hesitate to compare our very lives to that lifeless coin. The coin, with an image of a king imprinted on it, has value but only if it is found. Other than that, it is lifeless; it cannot move, and certainly it cannot find its own way back. We too can find ourselves spiritually lifeless and incapable of any movement. We too forget that we have an image of the one who gives us our being and life imprinted on our hearts. And we too need help from that Godly presence and each other to help sort through the dust of our lives, to feel and see again, to be home again and to know who we are born to be, and to whom we belong.

In our lives, most of us have had glimpses of who we are in God or who God wants us to be. I know I have, and yet, it hasn't always been easy to respond and commit to that. Still, when I look back and reflect, I know that God was there, during my childhood, making himself visible in the faces of the heroic priests of my youth in Poland who protested totalitarianism because they knew that saying yes to God has to mean also saying no to everything in this world that violates God's love and justice. Some of them, including our parish priest, paid for it with their lives.

God was also there letting himself become known to me when, as a child, scared of all the chaos and violence that was taking place in Poland as the totalitarian state was collapsing, I felt called to assemble a home altar and mimic what I saw priests do in church: say mass, and feel that even though everything around me was falling apart, I was being held by this Motherly presence of a loving God capable of dissolving my fears.

And God was there calling me by name when, on a busy Indian street, after I went to India thinking, like many others, that I would be able to get closer to God in the silence of some remote Himalayan monastery, God showed up on the street and she grabbed me by the hand and asked me to accompany her on her journey of healing and hope. This time God had the face of a thirteen-year-old homeless child; her face burned with cigarettes; her body bought and sold many times; and her conscience nearly killed by the heartlessness and abuse of countless men. It is that child that brought me to the community I told you about at the beginning. I went there convinced that I was going to make a difference and help find those who are lost. But instead, it is I who was served. It is I who was found. It is I who was given new life.

Before that day, I was a lost sheep. I was a lost sheep making my own plans, always caring about God but imagining my own ways of getting closer to and serving him. And most of it had very little to do with God. I was just wandering from one patch of grass to the next, and the grass always seemed greener wherever I was not. But there came a time when the aimless wandering had to stop because Christ in the form of a homeless child showed up and knocked on the door of my heart and asked, *May I come in? Do you have any space for me there?*

From then on he began walking with me. His wounds became a mirror for my own wounds. Like those crawling, limping, walking siblings rescued from the streets, there was no reason to pretend that I was more than I actually am. There was no need for niceness and pretense, no need to waste time on anything that is not a real cry of the heart. After all, as Henri Nouwen said, "Fruitfulness comes out of brokenness."[1] And, like soil that becomes fruitful when you break it up with the plow (Matthew 13), we too can only receive God's gift and life when we name the need for it.

It is for this reason that all the sheep in the parable are meant to move together and stay in their fold. We too are meant to travel together, with each other, in community, mirroring to each other what Christ would want us to see in ourselves. Together we can learn how to take off our masks and be who we really are. Together we can help each other see and celebrate. Together we can give each other strength and learn how to take turns holding each other's pain. Together "we keep on returning to those we belong with who keep us in the light." Together we can not only say yes to God's constant searching for us but can join the search and become part of the rescue team.

I find these images of the lost sheep, the lost coin, and our Motherly God tirelessly helping us sort through the dust of our lives most helpful. These images help us, as contemplative activists, to see who we are meant to be and why we are here. As we meditate upon them and relate them to our own lives, I ask you: How are you being called today? Where do you find yourself on the map of lost and found? How have you found the places that are home for you? And how are you home for others, who come and are longing to be affirmed, cared for, and seen?

PART ONE

Listening to Life

CHAPTER 1

To Be Human Is to Revolt against Injustice

A few years ago, I was in Upstate New York co-facilitating a retreat for homeless youth. We were there for a few days of praying, reflecting on our lives, and experiencing the beauty of the surrounding environment. For many of the kids who came, this was their first opportunity in a long time to sleep in a comfortable bed, and they took the time to rest. My role at the retreat was to meet with every participant for one-on-one pastoral conversations and spiritual direction in between the usual retreat activities. One of those conversations is still very much with me today.

On that day I was meeting with everyone outside the chapel, surrounded by a pond, flowers, and trees. I sat there quietly, reading, praying, and once in a while one of the retreat participants would come to sit with me. I started each meeting with a brief guided meditation, and then we moved into a conversation.

A young girl named Ebony approached me there by the chapel. Painful things from her past were beginning to come up for her during the retreat, and she had difficulties expressing them. Seeing her pain and how difficult it was for her to give words to her years of private suffering, I encouraged her to go for a walk around the chapel and try to find three objects in nature that represented some of what she was feeling. She came back after about twenty minutes, and I asked her to talk about each of the objects and why she picked them.

One of Ebony's objects was a flower that had yet to bloom. She told me that she felt like this flower, like there was a gift inside of her trying to emerge, but no one knew. Even she had forgotten it. She said, "I am like this flower. From the outside no one knows that this flower has the potential to be beautiful, to offer fragrance, and to bloom, unless they look inside. One day I know I will bloom, but I don't seem to be able to get there."

I was struck by the truth in her words. There clearly did exist within her beauty, potential, and heartfulness, but it was all hidden and guarded by the rigid pain of her past. After talking about this for a while and feeling somewhat helpless in my inability to offer her any consolation, I suggested to Ebony that she take her three objects and go into the chapel and spend some time in prayer and meditation. She went in, closed her eyes, and meditated for some time in silence while holding her objects in her hands.

She was the last person on my list to see that afternoon, so I left my spot while she was in the chapel and went to get some tea. Sometime later I noticed her from a distance running toward me with a big smile. I wasn't sure what had happened, but I noticed that she was radiant with life.

"What is it?" I asked.

"Look at this flower," she answered.

I looked at the flower and indeed it was beautiful, but I didn't notice anything unusual.

"It is the same flower that I showed you earlier," she said. "I was holding it in my hands while praying with my eyes closed and I felt something. I felt like all those struggles that I was feeling but was unable to express in words just kind of dissolved, and there was this sense of relief and peace. When I opened my eyes, I was shocked. The flower that I had held in my hands opened and bloomed while I was praying."

Witnessing her words and radiant face, I felt like something special had just happened. Years later, she said that this little flower meditation, as she called it, was the starting point of a new life for her. It gave her permission to emerge out of hiding and to say yes to the gift that she was carrying in her heart, the gift that was hers to give to the world.

The story of creation in Genesis 1, among other things, points to the possibility of something special and unique in each of us—exactly what Ebony intuited in herself during that retreat. It says that we were all created in the image of God, and therefore at the core of our identity and destiny lies something that has the imprint of God written all over it. Some of the early spiritual masters of our tradition elaborated on this further. Gregory of Nazianzus told us that during the creation, "God took a lump of newly created earth, formed it with his immortal hands into our shape, and . . . breathed into it a flash of the invisible godhead." Origen told us that humans are no small thing because within each of us there is "the whole universe in miniature . . . with sun, moon, and stars, too." Pseudo-Macarius compared human beings to "countless lamps" burning with the brightness of God because we "were all lit at the same holy fire." In more recent times, the great Black theologian and spiritual writer Howard Thurman taught that "There is in every person an inward sea, and in that sea there is an island, and on that island there is an altar" and that spending time there is our "crucial link with the Eternal."[1]

All of this is so beautiful, so poetic and mystical. But what does it mean? How does it relate to the practical? How can this help us to deal with the realities of our lives and our world?

A contemporary Jewish scholar, Rabbi Shai Held, commenting on Genesis 1, says that "in the ancient world, various kings (and sometimes priests) were described as the images of God. It is the king who is God's representative or intermediary on earth, and it is he who mediates God's blessings to the world. In dramatic contrast to this," he continues, "the Bible asserts that ordinary human beings—not just kings, but each and every one of us—are mediators of divine blessing. The entire race collectively stands vis-à-vis God in the same relationship of closeness and protection that characterizes the god-king relationship in the more ancient civilizations of the Near East."[2]

Clarifying this point further, Rabbi Held acknowledges that many of us struggle with the idea of viewing ourselves and our human affairs through the lens of royalty. Monarchy, after all, has long been an abusive institution whose very survival depends on the exploitation of its vulnerable subjects. If there is anything that our world needs less of, it is that. But here, Rabbi Held insists that what the biblical story of creation proposes is not just a simple replication of that "ancient Near Eastern royal ideology," but "a radical democratization" of it. If we are all kings and queens, as the Bible seems to assert, then the idea of some of us ruling over others shifts drastically because, "If everyone is royalty, then on some level, when it comes to the interpersonal and political spheres, no one is." Positions of power, then, are envisioned in terms of their responsibility "to nurture and protect" and "not a license to abuse and exploit."

In support of this, both the prophets (see Ezekiel, for instance!) and the psalmist are clear, again and again, in their message to the powerful: their work is to serve and empower people in their care, and not just to care about their own welfare.

It is for this reason that James Cone, the father of Black liberation theology, connects this idea of a reimagined royalty to the human freedom to revolt against oppression. He says that being created in God's image and likeness "means that human beings are created in such a way that they cannot obey oppressive laws and still be human. To be human is to be in the image of God—that is, to be creative: revolting against everything that is opposed to humanity." To be created in the image of God and to embody the likeness of God, therefore, is not just to accept the mystical dignity that comes from knowing that we were quickened with the "flash of the invisible godhead" but also to know the task and the purpose connected to it. The God we worship and are made in the image of is not a static God of keeping things as they are. The God we worship is the God of life, the God of Exodus, the God who leads people out of the house of bondage and into freedom. Not just inner freedom but freedom that is also social and political. And, in the world in which people, whole groups of people, are oppressed, the image and likeness of God are "the [very] humanity involved in the . . . struggle against the forces of inhumanity."[3] So the forces of death can be dispelled, and so the healing forces of life can become our hope and our new reality.

On the day of the retreat that I mentioned at the beginning of this chapter, that young homeless girl, Ebony, got her first glimpse of what her life could be when she sensed that she too was destined to be "burning with the brightness of God." That was the start of her new life. That gift or grace gave her permission and energy to do the work she needed to do, to find the right support, and ultimately to take on the world that often wasn't on her side.

We, too, in the light of what's happening in our world, need to move from just knowing that God is imprinted on our hearts to actually saying yes to how this imprint can dictate how we live. We need to remember that each of us was created in a way that not only encourages but requires us to oppose injustice in any and all forms, if we are to stay human, if we are to continue to be God's lamp for this darkened world.

To be alive and awake right now, in this time in history, is to see clearly the ongoing pattern of injustice and racism present in our country's very DNA. As we wake up each day—to paraphrase the words of one of the bishops of the church—may we be reminded that our tradition tells us that Christ often comes to us crucified and powerless, and that in America, Christ often shows up as tortured, Black, and lynched. When he knocks on the doors of our hearts, we need to try and say yes to him, knowing that saying yes to him means saying yes to our own humanity.

CHAPTER 2

Prayer Is Like Talking to an Empty Chair

I once heard the story of an elderly man who was facing the end of his life.[1] This man's daughter, knowing that her father wasn't really a churchgoer and feeling somewhat concerned about the well-being of his soul, asked the local priest to come and pray with her dad. When the priest arrived, he found the man lying in bed with his head propped up on two pillows and an empty chair beside his bed. Seeing the empty chair the priest said, "I guess you were expecting me?"

"No, who are you?" the man answered.

"I'm the new parish priest," the pastor replied, "and your daughter asked me to stop by. When I saw the empty chair, I figured you knew I was going to stop by today."

"Oh yeah, the chair," said the bedridden man. "Would you mind closing the door?"

Somewhat puzzled, the priest shut the door.

"I've never told anyone this, not even my daughter," said the man, "but all of my life I have never known how to pray. At Sunday Mass, I used to hear the priest give sermons about prayer, but it always went right over my head. When I confronted the priest and told him that I couldn't make any sense of his teachings on prayer, he gave me a book that was supposed to be the best book ever written on contemplative prayer. The book was so abstract that after reading a few pages I gave up and abandoned any attempt at prayer. It just seemed beyond what I was capable of. And then one day a few years ago my best friend said to me that prayer is just a simple matter of having a conversation with God."

"Here's what I suggest," he said. "Sit down on a chair, place an empty chair in front of you, and in faith see Christ on the chair. It's not spooky because Christ promised, 'I'll be with you always.' Then just speak to him and listen in the same way you are doing with me right now."

"So, I tried it and I liked it a lot. In fact, this practice of talking to God and listening to God became so meaningful to me that I now practice it for a couple of hours a day. This is especially helping me now when I am often in pain, dealing with my aging body and the uncertainty of what tomorrow will bring. I get a real sense of God's presence from this. I feel like Christ is really with me these days."

That story of the elderly man on his deathbed talking with the priest has always stuck with me, and it resonates with another teaching I was given.

One of the greatest lessons in my life about prayer came from a renegade rabbi who spent decades working on the streets of New York City rescuing kids from homelessness and prostitution—a holy man who dedicated his life to seeking God in the darkest shadows of Manhattan. He helped to make prayer real by giving me these simple instructions: "When you pray, talk to God just as if you were talking to your best friend. Tell the Holy One everything. Especially, dedicate specific times each day when you tell God about all your worries, all your hurts, all of your problems. Take off your mask and just speak. If you do that, if you really let your whole essence speak to God like that, some days there will be a lot of tears. But that's a good thing. And when you are done telling God about your hurts, when there are no more words to be said and you are completely spent, just silently rest in God, letting God hold you. And then for the rest of the day practice joy and optimism knowing that you are God's beloved child, knowing that you are loved, and knowing that you are carrying a great gift in your heart. Then when sadness sweeps again, spend time telling God about it only to be able to transition into joy and aliveness, confidence and trust."

In some of the most difficult times in my life, this way of prayer is what saved me—telling God everything, crying with God, wrestling with God, and then when all is said and done, just resting in God, feeling loved into newness, feeling loved into aliveness and joy.

This Jewish teaching on prayer is very much at the heart of our Christian contemplative tradition, too. Saint Teresa of Avila, a sixteenth-century Spanish Carmelite nun who had a tremendous influence on contemporary spirituality, defined prayer as "an intimate sharing between friends." She said that prayer does not have to be very abstract, difficult, or esoteric. Prayer is as simple as developing human friendships. It is, she said, "taking time frequently to be alone with the One who we know loves us."[2] It is talking, it is listening, it is delighting in God's presence. It is telling God our secrets and inviting God to tell us his own. It is, at times, resting in God's arms and asking to be held; it is making space for depth, intimacy, and deep sharing. Also, at times, it is about having frank conversations, about wrestling with things that need to be named and addressed, things that at first feel like they could damage the friendship, but in the end always prove to deepen it and move us from safe but inauthentic peace to real communion.

And as months and years continue, we get to the point in our prayer practice where perhaps we have less to say to each other, where our very gestures speak more than words, and where we can embody the gospel mandate to pray always, even if quietly. It is not that we constantly are saying our prayers. It's more that, like a mother who even when away from her child has a physical sensation of their presence, and all her words and actions in some way or form are done in relation to that child's well-being, so we, too, are walking through life with that constant awareness of the One who loves us, the One who helps us carry our burdens, the One who envelops us in his love like a comfortable blanket and gives us strength.

As with human relationships, our relationship to God has to start with us dedicating some time each day to building that bond. Prayer is the ground where distant familiarity becomes friendship, where friendship becomes communion, and, with time and attention, where words become a deep silence that speaks and loves.

So, now, I invite you to spend a few minutes in silence practicing this way of prayer. The rest of the book will wait. You might simply grab a chair, see Christ there, and talk to him. Pour your heart out as if to a friend.

CHAPTER 3

Don't Try to Be Mother Teresa or Saint Francis

There I was, lying in a dark room covered with a blanket, and my whole body was shaking with fear. The priest I often saw in church, Father Stanisław Suchowolec, had just been found dead in his church apartment, within walking distance from where I was. His was the second unexplained death of an activist priest in the last ten days. Immediately after it happened, stories began circulating in the official newspaper of the state, saying that it was an accident. We all knew, though, what had really taken place; he was killed by the government in their latest attempt to teach us a lesson about who was really in charge. A chaplain of the banned pro-democracy Solidarity movement in my native Poland, he was one of the last victims of the totalitarians in charge, just months before their power was taken away.

Father Suchowolec had been receiving death threats for a long time. He was the activist and spiritual successor to another priest, his best friend, Father Jerzy Popiełuszko, who was once described by John Dear as a "simple, shy, devout priest—but also a towering prophet and mighty nonviolent resister, the Martin Luther King Jr. of Poland."

Father Popiełuszko was a priest known not only for attracting thousands to his "mass for the nation," which took place every month in his church in Warsaw, but also for his more private self—offering love and a gentle disposition toward others, including those who were eager to take his life. It was not uncommon for him during the Polish "martial law"—or "state of war" as we called it—to leave the church refectory, where he lived and was safe, to bring hot coffee and food to the secret police stationed outside watching his every move. He did not want them to have to sit hungry and cold for hours at a time. Some laughed at him; some responded to his gestures with tears, and some asked him to receive their confession, right there on that cold street, as they begged God for forgiveness of the evils in which they were complicit. But, almost universally considered a holy man by those who knew him, Fr. Popiełuszko too was killed, a few years before Fr. Suchowolec. His body, beaten, broken, and deformed, was later shown on Polish national television, perhaps to show what happened to those who did not obey the totalitarian machine.

When I look back at my childhood, I know that the stories of these two priests, these two martyrs, infused me with something. By the time Fr. Suchowolec was killed, I was so deeply—though perhaps unconsciously—identified with the archetype of the priest, that on that night, as I lay terrified in my bed, covered with a blanket, my childhood psyche imagined that the bad guys who killed him were coming for me next. Their lives and their message continued to grow in me and help me see what my life needed to be; not another version of them, but in some way like them, a life of listening and responding to the quiet voice of God that calls each of us to an ever-greater freedom to say yes to love.

I think of all of this especially each year when we celebrate the Feast of the Presentation of our Lord, a feast commemorating an event in which the gift of a special kind of seeing is granted and things are recognized for what they are. This is the feast, also sometimes called Candlemas, during which candles are blessed so that our steps might be illumined and directed by the light of Christ. It is the feast during which we have a chance to learn again, or maybe see for the first time, who God is and who we need to be in response.

As the story goes, forty days after his birth, Jesus was brought to the temple in Jerusalem and placed in the arms of an elderly priest named Simeon. As the wise priest held this small child, getting ready to present him to God, something happened, and he suddenly realized that it was not he who was presenting the child to God, but that he himself was being presented.

We are told that on that day Simeon saw salvation. He held salvation in his arms. On that day, his decades of waiting were brought to an end, and his life was made complete.

According to some traditions of the church, this old man Simeon was blind at the time when this took place. He was blind, and yet he saw, not with his physical eyes but with the eyes of his heart. He saw with his whole being. Each year when we remember this special day, as we are getting ready to bless candles whose light will help us see and direct our steps for the rest of the liturgical year, we too are being invited to see. To see so we can know the way. To see so we can return back home. Home, back to ourselves. Back to that place from which there is no escape. Back to our problems but also back to our gifts. Because it is there, in our lives, that God wants to meet us. Not somewhere else. Just like two thousand years ago when God sent his Son to reach us through our all-too-human circumstances, problems, and gifts, now too, he is there waiting.

Christian spirituality tells us that the goal for all of human life is to become saints. What sometimes it fails to say is that you and I are not meant to become another St. Paul, or St. Francis of Assisi, or Mother Teresa. You are called to be you. And I am called to be me. We are called to become who God created us to be. As Fanny Brice, the great singer and actress of the 1930s said, you need to "Let the world know you as you are, not as you think you should be, because sooner or later, if you are posing, you will forget the pose, and then where are you?"

Or, a contemporary spiritual writer puts it like this: "Too often we short-circuit God's plans for our own holiness by comparing ourselves to some other saint or saying that we can't possibly be a saint in our own daily lives. People say, 'I'm just a student.' 'I'm just a teacher.' 'I'm just a grandparent.' But you're not 'just' anything, because God has created you as a beautiful and unique person. So, you're called to be a saint in your own way. As the Trappist monk Thomas Merton said, 'For me to be a saint means to be myself.' So maybe it's time to stop trying to be like someone else. Stop

looking at someone else's road map to holiness. Because all
the directions you have are inside your heart. As St. Francis
de Sales said, 'Be who you are and be that perfectly well.'"[1]

But to do that, to take that kind of a stand in our lives, to
claim who we are, takes a lot of courage. It also takes some
discernment and skill. It takes a special kind of seeing. A
seeing that can help us separate fiction from facts in our
lives. It takes the kind of seeing Simeon received on the day
of the Presentation. It takes the ability to see with the heart.

In our tradition, one of the saints who specialized in
helping people gain this kind of seeing was St. Ignatius of
Loyola. After facing some of his own illusions about who
he was meant to be, after separating fiction from facts in
his own life, he developed a methodology, an elaborate process, for being able to see clearly who we are in God and
how to be just that. He called this process "a discernment of
spirits." And while his process is quite elaborate and should
only be undertaken with the support of a proper spiritual
guide, he has two points of advice that I have found helpful
in my own life.

The first one is a meditative exercise in which we are
invited to imagine ourselves at the end of our lives, on our
deathbed, or even after our death, facing Christ and reflecting in his presence and light the regrets we have about our
lives. Being in that imaginative place and allowing ourselves to see our lives in that way, we simply ask ourselves:
What kind of person have I been? What kind of person have
I failed to become? What was the task that God brought
me here to do? What kind of thing was I born to fix in this
world? And, have I done that?

When I am faced with doubts and confusion about things and decisions in my life, I bring them into this practice. The result is always the same. Clarity.

Once we get clarity and are able to see and commit to the guidance we've received, St. Ignatius recommends that we ask God for signs to reassure us that we indeed are on the right path. And for Ignatius, one of the surest signs that we can ever receive from God is a sense of internal peace. Peace . . . that feeling of rightness that we sometimes experience when we make the right decision.

Another possible sign, I would suggest, is the kind that is present in the Gospel passages we typically read on Presentation Sunday. I am talking about more than Simeon and his realizations and experience. In that same passage of Luke 2, in which Simeon glimpses salvation, I am struck by how many signs are recorded. There are individual intuitions and dreams. But there are also events at which people show up in the life of the holy family only to remind them of what Jesus's identity and mission are and how they are to support it. For example, Luke 2 says,

> And the child's father and mother were amazed at what was being said about him. Then Simeon blessed them and said to his mother, Mary, "This child is destined for the falling and the rising of many in Israel, and to be a sign that will be opposed so that the inner thoughts of many will be revealed—and a sword will pierce your own soul, too." There was also a prophet, Anna, the daughter of Phanuel, of the tribe of Asher. She was of a great age, having lived with her husband

seven years after her marriage, then as a widow to the
age of eighty-four. She never left the temple but wor-
shiped there with fasting and prayer night and day. At
that moment she came, and began to praise God and
to speak about the child to all who were looking for the
redemption of Jerusalem. (Luke 2:33–38)

We too, sometimes, need to be reminded by others. By
those who can see into our hearts and the heart of God. We
need to be reminded who we were born to be and what our
lives need to be about. Because our world is full of messages
about the ideal lives we should have. But we are not called
to have ideal lives. We are called to live and fully occupy our
own lives right where we find ourselves.

This Feast of the Presentation takes place, also, as we
continue to follow the Epiphany glow of Christ's light, and
then is followed soon afterward, as we enter the season
of Lent, in which we are invited to walk in darkness, not
because of the absence of God but so we can develop our
spiritual senses to see God in places where God seems hidden. We live through all of this, every year, in church and
out, as our lives are full of infusions of light, followed by
what feels like searching in darkness. How do we make
sense of it—where we stand, where we are?

I invite you to join me in reflecting on who God wants
us to be. In doing so, don't be afraid to utilize the advice of
St. Ignatius and imagine yourself on your deathbed facing
God. I promise you, if you approach this exercise whole-
heartedly, some things about your life and your own way

to holiness will become crystal clear. And then, have some heart-to-heart prayerful conversations about your discoveries with a friend or two, the kind of friend who you know understands your heart.

The truth is that you and I have been created and called to be someone really special. You and I have been created and called to be ourselves. It is only out of the material of our own selves and lives that we can build a frame in which God can make a home. It is only through our lives that God can live, act, and love in humanly recognizable ways. It is only there that the reason for why we were born into this seemingly broken world, and the task we are here to complete, can be discerned and known.

I hope we don't wait until we face the end of our days and are then paralyzed by our regret. Instead, I hope we all choose to return home today. Home, to our own bodies, to our own minds and hearts. Home to our own circumstances and lives. I hope that we return home and invite God for some heart-to-heart time.

CHAPTER 4

Searching for Answers in the Mountains of New Mexico

I spent some time recently walking in nature in total silence. It reminded me of a time many years ago that was very significant in my life.

In 2005, before beginning my work with homeless youth in New York, I went to spend time with a Native American elder named Bear Heart in the mountains of New Mexico.[1] Bear Heart was one of those special people, one of the last living elders trained traditionally by his tribe to be a medicine man. He was also a Baptist minister, as it often was with Native Americans who had to live in two worlds. In him, many worlds came together.

I went there to see him so he could guide me in a vision quest, a time alone in the mountains with no food, no water, no fire, no tent, no cell phone. It was a time of prayer, fasting, and emptying myself so I could better attune my soul to hear and sense the "light and whisper" of God's guidance in my life.

My time in the wilderness was full and rich. Of course, there were aspects that were terrifying, especially that first night alone as the sun set and the forest darkened and I heard the sounds of the wild animals draw close. It was I who was the visitor in their home.

But the longer I stayed, the more I accepted that the only way to get through the experience was to say yes to whatever may be. The more I said yes to it, the more my heart opened to a gentle guidance that came and whispered an invitation to the great feast that our lives can be in God.

That time in the mountains marked a new beginning for my life.

At the conclusion of my vision quest, the holy elder pronounced a blessing over me. He looked at me and said that even though I might have thought that I decided to come to visit him, I was, in fact, destined to be here from the beginning of time. Just like St. Paul, who on his way to Damascus had his conversion experience, the elder told me that what I had lived during the vision quest was my Damascus experience. This was my initiation, the beginning of my work in the world.

From then on, Bear Heart said, I was to walk with wolves, those whom the world perceived as dangerous and not worthy of love, and yet, for those who are able to get close to them, are capable of great affection and care. In my life, I was to walk with those whom the world fears, even as they carry within them a potential for great goodness and great love. It would be my work to help them become that. The elder also said that I should never do my work or ministry for acknowledgment or fame. I was to do it because God assigned it to me. Finally, I was given a Muskogee-Creek name, meaning "Merging into One Spirit," which I was to use to address my creator, and my life was to be a continual return to the place of stillness deep within, the place I experienced while fasting and praying in the mountains, the place available to all, where God's tender care can be felt and known and from which we are sent into the midst of human suffering and indifference, to be God's partners in transfiguring the world.

Whether we perceive it or not, the invitation to enter into God's presence is always extended to us.

In the Parable of the Wedding Feast (Matthew 22:1–14), Jesus compares the kingdom of heaven to a king who gives a wedding banquet for his son. The original guests react poorly to their invitations, some brushing it off saying they're too busy with other matters, and others going so far as to kill the servants sent to fetch them. The situation escalates quickly; the king is outraged and sends soldiers to kill the guests who murdered his servants and to burn down their city. The king then commands his servants, saying, "The wedding is ready, but those invited were not worthy. Go therefore into the main streets, and invite everyone you find to the wedding banquet." The servants then go out and gather everyone who will come, the ragged and the well-dressed, the "worthy" and the "unworthy"; and the wedding hall is soon filled with guests. But what happens next is startling. When one guest is discovered without the appropriate wedding garment, he is expelled with somewhat violent words. The king commands: "Bind him hand and foot, and throw him into the outer darkness, where there will be weeping and gnashing of teeth. For many are called, but

few are chosen," Jesus summarizes, at the end of the story
(Matthew 22:13–14).

Read literally, this parable may convince us that the God
of the Bible is one of the most unpleasant and emotionally
unbalanced characters in all of the world's literature.[2] But,
things are never that simple. Flannery O'Connor offers us
some guidance—"In the land of the dead," she says, "one
often needs to scream to wake people up." Is Jesus exag-
gerating in order to get our attention, to make an important
point? Reading the parable from this lens, we can understand its hyperbole as less about revealing a capricious
God, and instead as a story meant to wake us up to a truth
we may otherwise ignore and miss.

What is that truth? God has invited each and every one
of us to the great feast that can be our life. It is a feast where
joy overshadows our normal worries and pains and where
the smallness of our lives is transformed into the largeness
of God's dream. It is a feast where each of us has a place to
sit, eat, drink, talk, and even dance, and where our wounds
are transformed into gifts. It's a feast that changes us into
the likeness of Christ, God's very heart, and where our lives
begin to echo the holy energies of God's compassion, which
our world needs so much right now.

But in order to hear and truly accept the invitation to this
feast in our lives, we need to do some work. We need to step
out of the matrix that normally governs our lives and listen
deeply to the heartbeat of God present in our hearts. How
we respond matters.

Returning to the parable, the guest who accepted the

invitation but showed up without a proper garment . . . his removal from the feast tells us that it is not enough for us to hear the invitation and come without any real prep work. It is not enough to show up and sort of pretend that we are there, heads in our phones as the food is served, making sure that we are accounted for but not really present. The yes in our lives needs to be wholehearted and complete otherwise we won't be able to partake in the joy that is available there; otherwise we won't be able to share the joy we have received with others. Our yes needs to be such that we do more than just worship Christ, and actually become a Christ.

So in a world of terrifying news, we can be the good news. Good news to those who are violated daily by human indifference. Good news to the least of our brothers and sisters. Good news to those who suffer from political calculations that do not include them. Good news to those hungry for our attention and love.

So one day, at the end of our days, when we come face to face with our God, God can look into our eyes and say, in the way I imagine God improvising Matthew 25:

> For I was hungry, and you gave me something to eat.
> I was sick, and you looked after me.
> I was a stranger and you welcomed me in.
> I was walking home and you didn't follow me. You
>   weren't afraid of me.
> I was being harassed on the train and you
>   intervened.

I came to this country as a refugee and you did not
   shut your doors.
I was wrongfully murdered, and you said my name.
My parents were taken by ICE and I was put in a cage
   and you went to court on my behalf, fighting for
   me.

During my time of fasting and prayer in the mountains of New Mexico, I received a glimpse of an invitation that God had for me, an invitation to a life of listening and saying yes. This was my Damascus moment. What are some moments in your life, your Damascus moments, when God has given you a glimpse of what your life needs to be about? And how are you responding to that call today? How are you saying yes, and where are you still resisting? What do you need to fully come to this feast that is your life? How do you need to claim God's gift and share it with others?

I hope that you will spend a few moments in silence . . . reflecting on this . . . inviting God to show you who you were born to be.

CHAPTER 5

Let Your Heartbreak Be Your Guide

A few years ago, I was invited to give a talk at an old church in London. This particular church had a very intriguing modern history: in the 1990s, it was bombed by the IRA. After being rebuilt, the bishop of London decided to turn it into a Center for Peace and Reconciliation. Today, it is a place for many young seekers who may not always feel at home in the church but who find a home in that particular one, as they seek a spirituality that can help them address some of the wounds of the world.

After my talk, a young woman approached and asked if she could speak with me. We went outside and sat on the floor of a big Bedouin tent located in the church's courtyard. She had some serious questions that she wanted to talk about, questions not so unusual for a person her age. Questions about what a young person is to do with one's life in our seemingly broken world. Questions about how to respond to everything that is not working in our world without feeling paralyzed by overwhelming worry. Questions about living with integrity and decency. Questions about our future, and the fact that sometimes it feels like the future is being stolen from our youth, by all of us who so willingly dismiss any dreams of a better tomorrow as impractical, as soon as we realize that any real societal change will require us to change.

And so, we sat there on the floor of that Bedouin tent and talked for a while. At some point in our conversation, as we talked about her specific vocation and calling, and how people often encouraged her to follow her passion and do what makes her feel good, I remembered the advice of one of my own mentors, Andrew Harvey. He said—and I'm sure he was responding to a famous bumper sticker from the 1980s still seen on many cars: "Don't 'follow your bliss.' Look at the world and see where following our bliss has gotten us to. Instead, follow your heartbreak." So that's what I said to that young woman that day in London: "Look at the world. What breaks your heart? And let your heartbreak be your guide."

I had mostly forgotten about that conversation until months later when I received a message from her. She said that she had sat with that "What breaks your heart?" question for a long time until she could not sit with it any longer. Somewhat frustrated, she turned on the TV and saw the stories of Syrian refugees arriving on the Greek island of Lesvos. Women, children, men, all scared and broken and some barely alive. Escaping the violence of war, hoping that they can survive the journey across the ocean, hoping for a new life. When she saw that, she knew that she needed to do something about it. Immediately, she got on the internet, bought a ticket, and without telling a soul, went to Lesvos the next morning to be there for those who were reaching the shores of the island. Being there broke her heart and brought her to her knees. But it also gave her a new life and a new joy. Not a false kind of joy that is the result of avoiding life's discomforts, but rather a joy that knows difficulties and heartbreaks and yet still survives. A joy that is an assurance that you are doing what you were born to do, an assurance that you are saying yes to the person you are meant to be. A joy that points to the truth of an old Hasidic teaching, that a person is only whole whose heart is broken.

This young woman eventually went back to London and helped organize her friends and colleagues at the church where we had originally met, helping to turn that church into a training center to prepare people to go and serve in refugee camps and become advocates for refugee families coming to the United Kingdom, who are otherwise often unwelcome there.

Advent, December, and Christmastime are heartbreaking for many of us, for often complicated reasons that go unsaid. Every year, I think of the familiar words of the prophet Isaiah that come up in the readings for Advent. The prophet reminds us that God is near. Isaiah says:

The Spirit of the Lord God is upon me.
The Lord has appointed me for a special purpose.
He has anointed me to bring good news to the poor.
He has asked me to proclaim comfort to those who
    mourn.
He has sent me to repair broken hearts,

And to declare to those who are held captive and
   bound in prison,
"Be free from your imprisonment!"
                              Isaiah 61:1, The Voice

It is for this reason, in the same spirit, that the Christian
message is called the good news. It is good news because
it is an announcement of joy to all people, especially those
among us who feel hurt and broken and who feel like they
don't belong. The season of Advent (leading up to Christmas), in fact, is about waiting for the coming of this good
news. It is a time of preparation when we are invited to sit
with everything in our lives that has not yet been touched
and transformed by and into this good news. We sit with
it in expectation, taking account of our joys and sorrows,
looking at what's wrong and what's right with our world,
learning to trust that God intends our wholeness, learning
to trust that even this darkness we are experiencing may
somehow be pregnant with light.

It was the theologian Matthew Fox who said:

There is grave danger . . . in sentimentalizing Advent
and Christmas and using these festival occasions to
look back exclusively at the birth of Jesus. Jesus was
born; he did live; he did teach as a rabbi would; he
did overturn frozen values of religion and society; he
did pay an ultimate price for doing so. But honoring
his birthday is, in my opinion, not the deeper meaning of Christmas and of its lead-in, Advent. To me, and

to many people before me, Christmas is not so much about the birth of the baby Jesus as it is about a birth going on in us. Hopefully. A birth of the Christ in us.[1]

One of the great medieval Christian mystics, Meister Eckhart, said something similar in the talks he gave frequently to nuns and others. One of his frequent themes was the greening, birthing essence and purpose of God, who wants nothing more than to be born in us.

So, sooner or later, each of us, like that young woman whom I met outside the once-bombed-out church in London, may discover a new life and a new joy. Perhaps when you echo the prophet Isaiah, it will include joy such as this:

The Spirit of the Lord is upon me because God has
    appointed me for a special purpose.
He sent me to preach the good news to those who are
    suffering in my neighborhood.
He told me to offer comfort to those whose lives and
    livelihoods were devastated by the pandemic.
He asked me to question and re-imagine our
    old tired systems that are based on violence.
He asked me to take a risk and be vulnerable with my
    community.
He told me that my heartbreaks can lead to joys.

CHAPTER 6

Remember Your Death and You Will Be All Right

Many years ago, I heard a story about an Indian priest and spiritual writer named Father Anthony de Mello. At one point in Father de Mello's life he met a rickshaw driver on the street in Calcutta. Apparently, the rickshaw driver was very poor and was in the process of dying from an excruciatingly painful disease. The man was so poor that he had even sold his skeleton to a local laboratory before he died, the only inheritance he would be able to leave for his children.

When Fr. de Mello first came face to face with this man, he was shocked. Not because of the man's poverty or sickness, but because of his complete lack of fear. The man's face radiated with freedom and aliveness, and he seemed completely at peace.

Somewhat confused by the man's peaceful countenance, de Mello asked him, "Aren't you afraid of the pain and suffering that is coming your way? Aren't you afraid of dying?" The man's face lit up, and with a gentle smile he answered, "Why would I be afraid? Today I am still alive and in touch with the joy of being able to breathe and see and feel things. Yes, there will be and already is pain, but I have complete trust in God, God who is life itself, and so there is really no need to fear anything."

Being in the presence of this poor rickshaw driver deeply impacted Anthony de Mello. Recalling this story later, he said that this one encounter had revolutionized his life, and he had never been the same since. He said: "Being with him, I suddenly realized that I was in the presence of a mystic who had reincarnated himself during this life. Being with him, I realized that I was in the presence of a holy man who had rediscovered life. He was alive; and it is I who was dead."[1]

Saint Paul's First Letter to the Thessalonians says, "The day of the Lord will come like a thief in the night" (5:2). In other words, he won't call ahead and make an appointment any more than a burglar would. He won't knock on our door to check whether we are ready.

Since I was a child, I have been intrigued by this imagery of God coming "like a thief in the night." This line, I believe, says something profound about how we ought to live our lives. What do we do when we think that a thief may show up at our door unexpectedly? What do we do when we know that an unannounced guest may come in the middle of the night? We definitely don't go to sleep. We stay alert, we prepare, we keep vigil, we listen expectedly, we pay attention. We stay awake!

Similarly, Fr. de Mello's encounter with the rickshaw driver became a defining moment, driving home the spiritual call to "stay awake!" He said: "Most people, even though they don't know it, are asleep. They're born asleep, they live asleep, they marry in their sleep, they breed children in their sleep, they die in their sleep without ever waking up."[2] The consequences of staying asleep are devastating. We miss a chance to be alive, to savor life. And we miss those encounters with God who consistently shows up in our lives in unexpected ways, just like God did with Anthony de Mello. So . . . let's not sleepwalk through life. . . . Let's keep our eyes wide open and ourselves alert (see 1 Thess. 5:6–8.)

How do we learn to stay awake and present to this gift that our life is? How do we learn to remember God's presence in our midst and trust in the way that rickshaw driver did?

Both Anthony de Mello's Ignatian wisdom and my Anglican tradition give us some good advice. The key to being awake, we are told, is to meditate on our death. This is one of the paradoxes of the Christian life: The more you remember your death, the better able you are to remember your life. This is not a teaching exclusive to Christians, either.

The American Buddhist Frank Ostaseski, who is also one of the pioneers of the hospice movement, said,

[L]ife and death are a package deal. You cannot pull them apart . . . [death] is the secret teacher hiding in plain sight. She helps us to discover what matters most. . . . Without a reminder of death, we tend to take life for granted, often becoming lost in endless pursuits of self-gratification. When we keep death at

our fingertips, it reminds us not to hold on to life too
tightly. . . . As we come in contact with life's precari-
ous nature, we also come to appreciate its precious-
ness. Then we don't want to waste a minute. We want
to enter our lives fully and use them in a responsible
way. Death is a good companion on the road to living
well and dying without regret.[3]

For the psychologist Abraham Maslow, this paradox of
finding life from death became ever more real after his own
near-death experience. "The confrontation with death," he
tells us, "and the reprieve from it—makes everything look
so precious, so sacred, so beautiful that I feel more strongly
than ever the impulse to love it, to embrace it, and to let
myself be overwhelmed by it. My river has never looked so
beautiful. . . . Death, and its ever-present possibility, makes
love, passionate love, more possible."[4]

Remembering your death helps you "keep your appointment with life," as Thich Nhat Hanh says. It helps you be
present to and appreciate the gift of the here and now.
Another spiritual teacher, Friar Brian Pierce, puts it this
way: "There is no place and no time outside of the present
moment for an encounter with God." To come home to God
"is to stand on holy ground—this ground, in this place, at
this very moment—and to know that . . . God is Holy Presence. God is the presence that presences itself within us and
around us. When we come home to the present moment, to
our deepest, truest self, we come to the One who whispers *I
am* with our every breath."[5]

I need to remember this and practice that remembrance with every breath I take. Life is too short and too beautiful to sleepwalk through it. Let's stay awake, pay attention, and keep our eyes open. I am convinced it is the only way to see God.

CHAPTER 7

Going into the Desert
of Our Hearts

It was Alice Walker who said,

> Some periods of our growth are so confusing that we
> don't even recognize that growth is happening. We
> may feel hostile or angry or weepy and hysterical, or we
> may feel depressed. It would never occur to us, unless
> we stumbled on . . . a person who explained to us, that
> we were in fact in the process of change, of actually
> becoming larger, spiritually, than we were before.[1]

We simply feel like we got stuck, like we stopped moving.
We may recall a sense of God's presence but now it is a thing
of the past. All we know now is dryness and thirst. All we
know now is hunger that accompanies those who get stuck
in the desert for too long.

The Gospel of John says that Christ is "the living bread
that came down from heaven" and that "whoever eats of
this bread" and tastes his presence "will never be hungry or
thirsty" (John 6:35 and 6:51). But how do we get to him? How
do we get to the nourishment that he offers? How do we see
our lives through his eyes? How do we recognize the gifted-
ness of where we are and know what steps to take next?

When ancient church fathers and mothers wrestled with these puzzling sayings from John's Gospel they often recalled the stories of Israelites wandering in the desert for forty years. They remembered that when Israelites struggled with hunger, God responded by raining down manna from heaven. They also remembered, however, the people's reactions to what they received and how somehow it was not enough. They remembered the complaints that this food was nothing like what they ate in Egypt. They remembered them murmuring about how their strength dried up because all they had to look at was this manna (Numbers 11:6). Refusing to accept that God would offer his people anything less than what they needed, one mystic, St. John of the Cross, concluded that the Israelites ate but didn't know the true nourishment they received because their spiritual senses were not awakened enough to register the extraordinary blessing they were given.

Christian mystics often connect St. John's "living bread that came down from heaven" to the Eucharist and the nourishment it offers. And with regard to that sacred meal, among Christians, similar things could be said of us as were said of the ancient Israelites and their manna. How often do we receive the Eucharist, and without being changed? Our spiritual senses are also too often asleep. One only needs to recall the words of the Vietnamese Zen master Thich Nhat Hanh to know how true this is. In *Living Buddha, Living Christ*, he wrote, "When we look around, we see many people in whom the Holy Spirit does not appear to dwell. They look dead, as though they were dragging around a corpse, their own body. The practice of the Eucharist is to help resurrect these people so they can touch the Kingdom of Life."[2]

So how can we wake up and see? How can we be nourished by the bread of life that Christ is and touch the Kingdom of Life? How can we come closer to the reality described by another one of our saints, St. Ambrose, who said that this "manna" of ours still rains down from heaven, even today, and that those who experience "this downpour of divine Wisdom" discover a new kind of awareness, a new kind of aliveness and delight, and a new sensitivity to God's presence in their midst.

Another of my favorite spiritual masters of the twentieth century is Catherine Doherty. Doherty died in 1985 and is not very well known today, but I think she should be, because she gave the Western church a real gift that she brought from her native Russia, a prayer practice called *poustinia*. This prayer practice, I believe, can help us wake up and truly see. It can help us to receive the spiritual nourishment that is Christ.

A little bit about Catherine before I explain her prayer method: She was born as a wealthy baroness in 1896 in Russia. Her family's position allowed Catherine to be raised in relative comfort, and at the age of fifteen she married a wealthy man. The 1917 Revolution forced her family to flee Russia, but they were captured by the communists at the Finnish border and nearly starved while being held there. Later they were rescued and eventually made it to Canada, where they experienced more hardship. Hunger, poverty, and destitution were their daily companions. To make ends meet, Catherine traveled alone to New York City, where she rented a piece of bed (meaning she shared a bed with two other women) and worked as a washerwoman and servant. She made pennies but managed to send much of what she made to her sick husband in Toronto. The ghost of starvation was always at her heels. Because, "when once you have really starved, you never really forget it . . . the kind of starvation . . . [when you are] too weak from not eating that you can't lift a finger."[3] But somehow she felt that the starvation she experienced in Russia was acceptable, because everyone was hungry. In New York, it was only the poor who were hungry, and no one wanted to do anything about it.

Sometimes she spent hours walking around restaurants where the rich and famous were dining, just so she could smell food and pretend that she was being nourished by it. The temptation to give way to prostitution was also very real, but she managed to resist it. "There are many saints in the slums," she later said. But extreme hunger made people do things that they would not normally do. She didn't think God became angry when people did things that circumstances like hunger and starvation pushed them into.

Eventually, Doherty managed to get a job at a shop where she met someone who worked for the Chattaqua Movement. Inspired by the stories of old aristocratic Russia that Catherine shared, Chattaqua hired her as a lecturer. Her new job was to travel around the country and give talks about pre-Revolution Russia. She was so good at it that eventually she became one of their more popular and well-paid speakers. Again she transitioned into a life of privilege and great prestige. Many even considered her a celebrity.

But as she regained a high socioeconomic status, her new

life began to bother her. "Did God allow me to escape Russia just so I could become rich and famous?," she asked herself. As she prayed about her life's direction and how God may be calling her to live, she recalled a nun she met in Egypt as a child. The nun showed her a statue of St. Francis and told her a story about this poor man of Assisi who gave up his wealth, gave what he had to the poor, and lived on the outskirts of his town. He even started hanging out with lepers, the very people who used to repulse him. Being with them opened Francis's heart and healed him. Being with them opened him to God and helped him come to terms with his own wounds.

Inspired by this, Doherty felt moved to follow in St. Francis's footsteps. With much prayer and the approval of a local bishop she gave everything she had to the poor and moved into a slum in Toronto. There her mission began, eventually leading her to build many centers of hospitality and friendship in the poor areas of different cities. She especially felt called to work with immigrants and challenge racism.

Seeking to integrate the contemplative depths of her Russian Orthodox background with her service in the West, she began to practice what she called "the way of *poustinik*." The word means "a hermit." This was a practice focused on spending time in solitude and living from a place of deep communion with God. Eventually this evolved into a teaching that she is most known for, her teaching on *poustinia*. It is this transformative practice that I think can lead to a greater connection with Jesus.

Poustinia is a Russian word that means "desert." And the practice of *poustinia*, in the deep vision of Catherine Doherty, encourages us to dedicate some time, perhaps one day a month or a weekend a month, in solitude, prayer, and fasting.

We go into a hermitage, and, mind you, a hermitage can be a room in your home or even a place in nature where you can be with God in silence. Once we are in our desert, we are freed from distractions. We fast only on bread and water. And the only book that we bring with us is the Bible, which we consult expecting that Jesus will use familiar words to offer us fresh wisdom. In this place of solitude and silence we open our hearts to God. We bring to God everything that is weighing us down. We voice problems, our hopes, our questions. We talk and then we listen. We listen to our frustrations. We listen to our joys. We listen to silence. And most of all we listen to the words of Scripture.

Much of the time in *poustinia* practice nothing may happen, and we may hear nothing significant. But if we stay long enough something will open up and guidance will come. If we stay long enough trusting the ancient teaching from the desert which says, "Go to your cell. Your cell will teach you everything," we will receive a word from God that is directed to us. A word in a form of an intuition, or a Scripture passage, or a feeling. We will recognize that word because it will feel like it is addressed to us directly, speaking to our difficulties, speaking to our questions, speaking to our joy. It will make us feel like our inner chaos was turned into something that resembles more order. It will infuse us with new energy and a new sense of hope and purpose. What was dead inside of us will begin to breathe again. And when we receive this word we write it down. We write down what God says to us and then do some more talking and listening.

Once we are done with our time of *poustinia*, we don't keep what we have received for ourselves. If we do that we may never receive it again. The word is always meant for us and for our community. So then we share it with our close spiritual friends; we share it with our community; we share it with our priest or spiritual director so together we can pray over it and discern what it means for all of us.

This is what Catherine taught, and the practice has changed many lives. It changed my life as I practiced it. I realized how easy it is for me, when I face challenges, to want to turn to external answers or quick fixes to cover up my difficulties. But that doesn't always work. In fact, it rarely works. What I need to do is go to my *poustinia*, to the desert of my heart (and a physical place which is, for me, special to this practice), bring all I am struggling with to God and sit and wait in trust. Christ always comes because that is his promise that he left with us. The promise is that we will never be left without support and guidance. This is the kind of practice that can help us establish a real friendship with God.

As St. Ambrose said, manna still rains down from heaven, even today. We only have to wake up and see. We only have to open our hearts and let that divine wisdom touch our hearts. Christ is the living bread, and he is eager to feed us with new life, new awareness, aliveness, and delight. We just need to make space in our lives for him. We need to make time for him; and I can say from experience, with the wisdom of Catherine Doherty, spending one day a month in prayer and fasting is a good way to start.

PART TWO

Touching What Frightens Us

CHAPTER 8

Sermon at Tanisha's Funeral

Today our hearts are broken, and we feel helpless and numb. The pain that we are feeling is making us doubt whether the work we committed to do here each day makes sense anymore. The work of rescuing kids who are forced to live on the streets of our city. Kids who are often forced to sell their bodies and souls for a sandwich or a place to sleep. Kids whose lives are marked by pain every day.

Today our hearts are broken because we lost one of those kids and witnessed a murder of a beautiful and precious teenage girl. A girl forced to run away from an abusive foster home. Run away . . . Run for her life . . .

A girl forced to grow up before she was ready to do so. Forced . . . Just so this could happen. So, a shot fired by an angry man could slash her heart. So, a shot fired by a pimp could kill her many dreams. So . . . she could breathe her last breath begging for mercy and help. So . . . she could lie there motionless covered with blood on that God-forsaken street.

I remember the night I met Tanisha for the first time very well. I was driving down Orange Blossom Trail in our outreach van like I do every night. And on that particular night the streets were very busy. It felt like all the old timers were there. There was Italian Mike. Crackhead Jimmy. And the whole Parliament House crew. There was Mama Sue and Michael. And like always they were all eager to share their burdens with us. Like always they asked for prayers and food.

And so there was nothing unusual there that night. Just another night of struggle and hustling. Just another night of people trying to do their best to survive yet another day. There was really nothing unusual that night except for this one new girl.

I remember seeing her from a distance. She was on another side of the street and the contours of her face felt blurry. But even from a distance I could see her BIG WIDE-OPEN brown eyes. Eyes that made me stop and think. Eyes full of longing. Eyes screaming for help. Eyes searching for a motherly love she never experienced but somehow knew that it is somewhere out there to be searched for.

And the word on the street was that she was only sixteen. A runaway from Michigan whose "boyfriend" put her out to work the streets so they could pay for a motel room and buy food.

The many times I met her I always had this feeling deep down in my heart that I needed to help her. I always felt this sense of urgency as if somehow I knew that we had a limited time. But there was just no way of reaching her guarded heart. The years of abuse she endured made it easier for her to get into strangers' cars than to trust someone who truly wanted to help.

Someone . . . who in her mind . . . was just another adult

capable of making promises and then doing what all other adults did to her . . . taking advantage of her vulnerability and destroying whatever was left of the child that lived inside of her.

But, over time, I saw her many times, and each time it felt like there was a little more trust.

Then, one day she was no longer there. She disappeared. We searched and worried and kept asking around. Initially no one knew anything. Then, we discovered she had been arrested for prostitution and was taken to the county jail. The feeling of urgency increased, and I knew that this was our chance. I had a clear sense that we had to go to jail and visit her. Unfortunately, this was against the rules of our agency. Making contact with any of the kids outside of normal street circumstances was forbidden.

But we still tried. We tried going to see her by engaging prison chaplains. We tried whatever we could. We tried because we knew that this was the time to convince her to come with us and stay at our shelter.

We knew this was the time to convince her that she needs to get help! But there was so much red tape. Appointments kept on getting postponed. And we didn't get to her in time. We tried and tried but we missed it.

Then, the night Tanisha was released from jail, she was shot and killed on a nearby street.

So here we are, today, gathering in shock and disbelief. Any life lost is a tragedy, but a life lost as a result of a brutal murder seems beyond what we can bear. A life lost is always a tragedy, but witnessing a life of a child, exploited, abused, and then slashed and killed is something that you and I never signed up for.

Funeral preachers are told that our job is to ease people's pain and put things in perspective. We are told that we are to preach hope. But, just like you, there is nothing in me right now that has access to anything that resembles hope. Like you, I feel broken and angry and I just want to scream. Like you, I have no words to ease anybody's pain. No words to ease my own pain.

Yet the doors of our center need to stay open, and we need to keep on showing up for other kids who may need us. The doors of our center need to stay open so what happened to Tanisha may never happen again.

Standing here in front of you I know that if there is any help to come it has to come from somewhere other than from us. It has to come from God. Because we have nothing. *Because we are completely spent.*

So I am asking you to gather your pain and join with mine. Let us do that, waiting on God to speak to us. Let us do that, hoping for an instruction that can turn these ashes we're sitting in into a garden giving us a glimpse of new life. Let us be here remembering the words Jesus spoke in John 6, where he tells us of his special mission from God, the "mission of losing nothing" and losing no one who was entrusted to him. He says this in the context of bringing back to life his good, troubled friend, Lazarus. There is no bone in my body that doubts that Tanisha is one of those special ones that Jesus especially cared for, as well.

As a wise spiritual teacher has said,

This mission of "losing nothing" is vividly pictured in the resurrection of Lazarus. He comes out of a tomb tied hand and foot with burial bands and his face covered with cloth. It is like he has been kidnapped and hidden away, lost to Jesus who loves him. Jesus finds him and demands he come forth from isolation. When he does, Jesus instructs, "Untie him. Let him go free." The kidnapping and confinement are over. He is back in relationship with the one who loves him. [Because] Love will not allow separation.[1]

I think that gathering here today we need to believe and remember that Tanisha too has finally been freed from her confinement and isolation. That the kidnapping—orchestrated by her life circumstances—is over and that she is finally released from the bands of abuse and that the cloth preventing her from seeing and experiencing true motherly love is removed. And that she is finally with the One who loves her.

She is with Her, embraced and welcomed. She is with Him, with every hardship she ever experienced tended to with care. She is with the Holy One, and her brokenness is finally transfigured into wholeness and joy.

So we should hold on to this hope and promise knowing that this joy of resurrection is also available to us. And that we can receive a spark of this joy of resurrection every time we come together like this, remembering Tanisha, remembering God, remembering that what dies will be one day raised and glorified.

CHAPTER 9

Our Global Dark Night

Do you remember the Gospel story of the disciples being stuck in a room frightened and perplexed after the death of Jesus? They might have heard about the resurrection, but they had not yet experienced it.

Sometimes it feels like our whole world is in this early post-resurrection phase. We know that the resurrection happened, but we have not yet seen it; we have not yet experienced it ourselves. So, we sit in a room with the door tightly barricaded. We sit in a room afraid. We sit in a room with the door locked hoping that no one will come and knock.

I'm not sure about you but I feel that way often. I look at the news these days and all I see is tragedy. There is Elizabeth Wathuti, a young Kenyan climate activist urging world leaders to "open their hearts" to the fact that over two million of her fellow Kenyans are facing climate-related starvation and that by 2025 half of the world's population will be facing water scarcity. There is a young vigilante with ties to the alt-right who after killing two people at a gathering protesting the shooting of an unarmed Black man by a police officer is acquitted of all of the charges, and three Republican politicians offer him an internship to celebrate his patriotism! And then there are all those mass shootings that seem to be happening almost every day now, like the one I just heard about when yet another desperate gunman couldn't take it any longer so he shot several people in a store only to then kill himself. And these are just some of many sicknesses that we are reckoning with during this time.

Clearly, we need help. We need something that can help us get through this. We need medicine for this sickness. We need a new way.

Saint John of the Cross, the sixteenth-century Spanish mystic, introduced a phenomenon into Christian spirituality called the "dark night" of the soul. It is a spiritual passage, an experience, or a trial that a seeker is to experience on their way to God if they are to get a real glimpse of who they are to become in God. It is really a divine gift that turns our self-made efforts into dust and moves us into surrender and trust.

The "dark night" is different from but not unlike depression. It is often experienced as a real failure at spiritual life and is normally accompanied by this sense of spiritual and psychological collapse and a total loss of God. What we held to be true dissolves, and meaning evaporates from our lives. The rug we stand on is pulled out from under our feet, and we are left with nothing to hold on to. The illusions of our control over our lives are unmasked, and all we can see is our inability to face the bigness of our problems. All we know is that the hope that guided us in our lives is not enough. We may continue to fight, but the darkness we are facing is simply too big and too deep for our own efforts.

John of the Cross tells us that this devastating experience—and "the dark night" is always devastating—should never be seen as a problem because it is a sign of spiritual progress. It is "a kind of initiation, taking us from one phase of life into another."[1] It is a solution to all of our failed solutions. It is an opportunity to claim our powerlessness so that God can be the real guiding and animating power in us. It is an invitation to make "the choiceless choice when the soul can do nothing but surrender."[2]

This is how Dr. Martin Luther King Jr. experienced his own passage from personal powerlessness to God's power in Montgomery on January 27, 1956, during the now-famous bus boycott. After receiving an anonymous phone call saying to him, "Leave Montgomery immediately if you have no wish to die," he got frightened. He hung up the phone, walked to his kitchen, and with trembling hands put on a pot of coffee and sank into a chair at his kitchen table. He described what happened afterward, in these words:

> I was ready to give up. With my cup of coffee sitting untouched before me, I tried to think of a way to move out of the picture without appearing a coward. In this state of exhaustion, when my courage had all but gone, I decided to take my problem to God. With my head in my hands, I bowed over the kitchen table and prayed aloud.
>
> The words I spoke to God that midnight are still vivid in my memory. "I am here taking a stand for what I believe is right. But now I am afraid. The people are looking to me for leadership, and if I stand before them without strength and courage, they too will fal-

ter. I am at the end of my powers. I have nothing left.
I've come to the point where I can't face it alone."

At that moment, I experienced the presence of
the Divine as I had never experienced God before. It
seemed as though I could hear the quiet assurance of
an inner voice saying: "Stand up for justice, stand up
for truth; and God will be at your side forever." Almost
at once my fears began to go. My uncertainty disappeared. I was ready to face anything.[3]

Dr. King provides us with an example of what can happen when, in the midst of despair, in the midst of helpless vulnerability, we accept our powerlessness. What first
appears like weakness actually becomes a gift that leads us
to surrender and trust. It becomes a gift that moves us from
self-effort to depending on God.

Now, St. John of the Cross and other mystics always
talked about this dark night as a personal experience. But
when I look at the world and our seeming inability to meet
the challenges we are facing, I wonder, is it possible that
what we are experiencing right now is something more
global—a dark night of humanity?

Dr. Richard Tarnas, a Buddhist teacher and depth psychologist, said the following about this:

I believe that humankind has entered into the most
critical stages of a death-rebirth mystery. In retro-
spect it seems that the entire path of Western civi-
lization has taken humankind and the planet on a
trajectory of initiatory transformation, into a state of

spiritual alienation, into an encounter with mortality on a global scale—from world wars and holocausts to the nuclear crisis and now the planetary ecological crisis—an encounter with mortality that is no longer individual and personal but rather transpersonal, collective, planetary; into a state of radical fragmentation, into the "wasteland," into that crisis of existential meaning and purpose that informed so many of the most sensitive individuals of the past century. It is a collective dark night of the soul, a deep separation from the community of being, from the cosmos itself. We are undergoing this rite of passage with virtually no guidance from wise elders because the wise elders are themselves caught up in the same crisis. This initiation is too epochal for such confident guidance, too global, too unprecedented, too all-encompassing; it is larger than all of us. It seems that we are all entering into something new, a new development, a crisis of accelerated maturation, a birth, and we cannot really know where it is headed.[4]

Tarnas concludes that, to get through this, "we can draw on those sources of insight that come from the mystical and shamanic epiphanies and writings of those individuals who have undergone a death-rebirth initiation." We can draw on our saints! And, "we can also draw from our own psychospiritual journeys, which perhaps permit us to glimpse that extraordinary truth which Goethe understood: "Until you know this deep secret—'Die and become'—you will be a stranger on this dark Earth."[5]

So perhaps we are experiencing a dark night that is not about our individual souls. It is about much more than that. And it is devastating. This darkness is leading to some necessary death, but, as our mystics tell us, with such death comes rebirth and new becoming.

Matthew Fox masterfully reminds us how "in a time of deep darkness, even 'lucky darkness,' there is little or nothing to steer by but the fire deep in our hearts . . . the fire that is hiding most deeply in our hearts. That is why the dark night can so readily bring out the best in us," and put us in touch with what's most genuine and real. It can help us to pay attention to that "spark of God" deep within, which we are to follow and learn from. Knowing that we are never left without guidance. Knowing that there are usually ways in which we need to cry out to God before guidance can come and before we can be ready to receive the help we need.[6]

What will die? What, if I may say so, *must* die before our struggling species can begin to be reborn? I imagine the answer to that question lies in our worship of everything unholy, our lust for unnecessary things, our pretending that those in need are far away, our excessive use of natural resources, and our willingness to live in silos, where only we and I and mine are safeguarded and of concern. Let all of this die. It was unholy and needed to die.

So no matter how the dark night comes to us, whether we are cowering in fear like the disciples of Jesus before they witnessed the resurrection for themselves, as we see the tragedies that the news brings to us every day, or through our personal pain, when the dark night comes, may it "knock loudly on the doors of our souls."

CHAPTER 10

Love in Times of Hate

Growing up in Poland, I was shaped by many stories about World War II that I heard over and over again as a kid. These stories were very alive for my grandparents who lived through the war, and also for my parents, who were born just a few years after the war had ended, and who grew up among the ruins of it.

The stories they told me created a sort of imaginary landscape of meaning in which I lived as a child. For example, there was a story of my grandfather's capture by Nazi soldiers who sent him to a work camp in Germany. There was also the story from my grandmother, who amid all the atrocities of war also talked about occasional acts of kindness shown her by the occupying army. And then there were these two, big, archetypal stories. Stories of special significance. Cruciform stories, if you will. Stories told on special occasions. Stories that signaled to us children that these were something to model our lives on.

The first of these was about a Franciscan friar, Father Maximillian Kolbe. Captured and taken to a concentration camp for his activities with the Polish resistance, he reminded us that "It is often in the darkest places . . . that light can shine at its brightest."[1] In 1941, when a prisoner escaped from the concentration camp he was in, as a punishment and to discourage future escape attempts, the head of the camp randomly chose ten men to be killed by starvation. As the guards picked out the last of the ten victims, the man chosen cried out in agony saying that he had a wife and eight children and that there would be no one to care for them once he was dead. Hearing that and moved by his words, Fr. Kolbe stepped forward and said that he had no wife and no children and that it was he who should be killed instead of the father of eight. The Nazi officer agreed to Fr. Kolbe's offer, and he was thrown into a cell with the other nine men and told laughingly that he and the others would "wither away like so many tulips." And when, after two weeks of starvation he was still alive, he would be given a lethal injection. Fr. Kolbe accepted his sentence calmly, and he died while praying, knowing that "Suffering for love, feeds love." The guard who went to posthumously examine his body reported that it was glowing with a strange light and that the cell was filled with the peace of holiness.

The second story was that of a Jewish doctor and famous children's author, Janusz Korczak,[2] who was known for taking care of Polish and Jewish orphans in Warsaw. His story too has a cruciform quality. Korczak had built several remarkable orphanages that functioned like little children's republics where orphan children had their own democratic government, court system, newspaper, and where each child's voice held the same value as that of an adult. On one August day in 1942, German soldiers came to his orphanage in the Warsaw Ghetto to collect his 192 children. As a well-known personality and author, Korczak was offered numerous chances to escape, including by a German officer who recognized him as the author of one of his favorite children's books. But Korczak refused, saying that he could not abandon his children.

Eyewitnesses tell us that, upon the arrival of the arresting officers, he gathered all the children, asked them to put on their best and most festive clothes, and together they formed a procession walking toward the train that took them to the concentration camp. As Korczak led the group out, holding a little orphan in his arms and followed by almost two hundred more, their procession radiated victory and celebration. It was as if they were walking toward the very altar of God. They walked peacefully with their heads raised high. They walked with dignity, with freedom. They walked like they already had won the war. It was as if they were saying to the Nazis, "You can kill us, but you can't kill our spirits. You can't kill love." People who witnessed that procession said that amid all the uprisings that they witnessed during the war, this was the most powerful act of resistance they had ever seen. There was something supernatural about this because even though they were marching toward death, they possessed life in a way that is rarely seen.

I am reflecting on these stories now, not only because they are fond memories of what my grandparents and parents taught me but because I believe these stories offer us a way out. A way out of the logic that our world operates on. A logic that lives inside of us and governs so many of our basic drives. A logic that led to the war these stories described and also, in some ways, is responsible for many of the heartbreaking things we are witnessing today. Personal and societal things.

This logic can be best summarized by what the philosopher Hegel called the "master-slave dialectic."[3] Applied to our societal history, it tells us that, when left to ourselves, we often organize our lives according to the principle of domination. Like two children fighting over a toy, we live to win because winning gives us meaning and fills us with a sense of security and power that we mistake for our real purpose. As a result, we often tell our story in a way where those who won are celebrated and those who lost are forgotten. Our history ends up being a story about the insiders, even though many of us end up as outsiders. And doing this, in many ways, is kind of normal, because what else can we do if we haven't yet been touched by the love of God and given a real sense of rootedness? What else can we do if we don't have a real place to stand? We simply go on hurting one another, trying to manipulate the whole world into reassuring us of our worth.

But our course can be corrected, and we can be relocated in what is our real purpose. When I think of this movement from what is to what could be, I am reminded of the mystery and meaning of the Paschal Triduum.

Starting with the evening of Maundy Thursday and moving through the crisis and hopelessness of Good Friday, and finally reaching its high point in the Easter Vigil, during the Triduum we are shown what Martin Luther King Jr. described when he said:

> We've been buried in numerous graves—the grave of economic insecurity, the grave of exploitation, the grave of oppression. We've watched justice trampled over and truth crucified. But . . . [on Easter we are reminded] that it won't be like that all the way. . . . [We are reminded] that God has a light that can shine amid all of the darkness.

Readings from the Hebrew Scriptures (mostly from Exodus 12) accompanying us during this period remind us of the Passover, when the ancient Israelites escaped slavery in Egypt, revealing that God has preferential care for the outsider and the powerless. Then in the Gospel reading for Maundy Thursday (from John 13) we see that real power is not the power of domination but rather the power of love. And, looking at life from the vantage point of love, we see that our being and our joy increase to an extent that we give it away. We see that the real significance of our lives grows the more we are willing to move beyond seeing others as threats and instead choose to delight "in their energy . . . [and] give away some of our own life to help resource their lives."[4]

All this is beautifully summarized in what our tradition believes Christ instituted on Maundy Thursday: the Eucharist. Where the other Gospels have Jesus speaking the words of the Institution, which says, "This is my body, this my blood," when Christ in a literal sense becomes our life-sustaining food and drink, John's Gospel has Jesus washing the disciples' feet. I hope that fellow Christians do not miss this. As contemporary spiritual writer Ronald Rolheiser explains, this "specifies what the Eucharist is in fact meant to do, namely, to lead us out of church and into the humble service of others."

"Eucharist," Rolheiser continues,

> is a call to move from worship to service, to take the nourishment, the embrace, the kiss, we have just received from God and the community and translate it immediately and directly into loving service of others. To take the Eucharist seriously is to begin to wash the feet of others, especially the feet of the poor.[5]

So, as we spend some time in silence before God as some of us do during the Triduum each year—a Christian's most holy time of the year—I hope that we also sit with these two stories I mentioned, which suggest what it means to follow God and what it means to be less, in order that others may become more. I hope that we reflect on what it means to share our lives and our privilege with those who have little or none. Enter the kind of darkness that we immerse in on Good Friday, entering the tomb, entering the earth, and eventually allowing God to be reborn in us so that we may truly live again.

And in this renewed state we might remember, "We should be on our knees washing each other's feet because that is precisely what Jesus did at the first Eucharist." Or, at least, be willing to die for one another.

CHAPTER 11

Another Good Friday?

"For weeks now it has been evening," Pope Francis remarked in his Urbi et Orbi (the Latin means "To the city [Rome], and to the world") address in 2020, during the initial days of the new and very frightening Covid-19 pandemic. All over the world, our streets were empty. Our stores were closed. We were confined and alone, and the sirens of ambulances were our constant soundtrack. When, on the rare occasions we risked stepping outside for some essential purpose, the gestures and glances of those we encountered, who upon seeing us from a distance usually chose to cross the street, mirrored our own fears and confusions.

Not unlike the disciples in the Gospel accounts, whose dreams were shattered by the reality of Jesus's arrest and crucifixion, we too were caught off guard by what we never imagined could happen, and were not quite sure what to do. We wanted to act, but were not sure how. We wanted to be helpful, but were told to stay home. We wanted to do anything to ease that sense of helplessness in us and maybe even in others, to feel like the stories coming out of our hospitals were simply not true.

Commenting on that, and connecting it to Jesus's arrest and crucifixion, Anglican priest and theologian Sarah Coakley says that medical professionals tell her that one of the key components of nursing training is learning what she calls "the discipline of staying." She says, "The doctors may come and go, fleeing if need be from what they cannot control or alleviate; but the nurses *stay*. They are taught this business of 'staying' to look on that which others cannot bear: the suppurating wound; the face horribly disfigured by burns; the gangrenous limb which awaits amputation; the agony of death itself."[1]

I see this movement—from a practical, solution-based way of doing, where we can feel that we have some control over what goes on, to a more passive way of being as one of the key lessons every Good Friday. While much of Jesus's public life and ministry has been about doing, commending, teaching, healing, and actively inviting people to taste and experience the miraculous presence of God in their midst, the moment his passion begins, all of his activity stops and he can no longer do things for others. Now, things are done to him, and "passiveness, non-activity, absorbing something more than actively doing anything" begin to define him. And strangely enough we are told that "we are saved more through Jesus's passion . . . [and passivity] . . . than through all of his activity of preaching and doing miracles."[2] Could it be that our situation today—with its many pandemics—calls for more of this kind of witness, of simply being with, no matter how hard, no matter how devastating?

Accepting this call to show up in this way is hard. We are

all tempted by a return to normalcy. We just want things to get back to how they once were. And while moving into the practical will have its time and place, the Good Friday experience is not about that. Good Friday is about the pain. Good Friday is about our helplessness. Good Friday is about joining Mary, at the foot of the cross, and witnessing with her all of our hopes being crucified and killed. Were we wrong? Were we fooled, or misguided? Was our hope entirely misplaced?

Good Friday is also about self-examination, remembering that, while what we are experiencing during times of crisis is not a punishment from God, it is a chance to re-evaluate our lives. Every crisis offers us this. This is an opportunity to seriously examine and wonder about all the shadows of our society's mindset that a crisis has revealed.

Those shadows, you know, all those things we see on the news almost daily these days, include our mixed priorities that favor profits over people, and our politicians who tell us that our elders shouldn't overburden our struggling system, that they should simply be ready to sacrifice their lives to save the economy. They include our constant refusal to acknowledge that our common life depends on one another's toil. They definitely include our increasing economic inequities; and, during the pandemic, they included our unwillingness to pay those who never stopped working because their jobs were considered essential, and if they had been allowed not to work they would have inconvenienced our lives of conveniences.

A Good Friday understanding is about looking at all of

these situations and asking ourselves: How much of this have we participated in and consented to? How much of this is done in our name? How much of this motivates how we live as individuals and in our communities? And are we ready to confess and ask God for forgiveness for the part we played in all of this? Are we ready to commit to change? The resurrection that we await isn't about returning to normal; it is about transformation. It is about change that you and I can commit to after this immense suffering.

The great Carmelite priest and spiritual director St. John of the Cross uses an image of a burning log of wood in one of his treasures on the mystical life to describe the way of the cross and the way to the resurrection that awaits a faithful soul.

> The soul is purged and prepared for union with the divine light just as the wood is prepared for transformation into the fire. Fire, when applied to wood, first dehumidifies it, dispelling all moisture and causing the wood to shed the tears it has held inside itself.
>
> Then it gradually turns the wood black . . . and even causes it to emit a bad odor. By drying out the wood, the fire brings to light and expels all those . . . unsavory accidents that are contrary to the nature of fire. Finally, by heating and enkindling it from without, the fire transforms the wood into itself and makes it as beautiful as it is itself. Once transformed, the wood no longer has any activity . . . of its own. . . . It simply possesses the properties of fire and does the work of fire.[3]

When we approach the darkness of Jesus's suffering and death and come to terms with the suffering of so many in our world today, we all may come to the light and experience the transformation that St. John of the Cross describes. We might remember that there is no resurrection without the cross and that the message of Good Friday is not to be strong but to be weak. The future may be about proclaiming the victory, but today is not.

To grasp Good Friday is to let go of our self-agency and lay our strengths at the foot of the cross. To let the circumstances we are experiencing work on us, squeezing out all that is not essential, and make space in us for God. We move from action to passivity and abandon ourselves into God's hands. Like the wood prepared for its task in the fire. We pray and weep and fast until we can honestly and truly say, "Not my will but your will," as Jesus said to the Father from the cross.

And the moment our hearts have the courage and readiness to pronounce those words, there will be very little left of us there. It seems to me, that is the goal of the Christian life. That is what Easter signifies for the journey of transformation that our souls are on. To cease to exist as we are so we may be brought into existence as God intends us to be.

Then, we have the opportunity to become more beautiful than we dare to be, and freer than our circumstances allow.[4]

CHAPTER 12

Learning to Follow God in a Refugee Camp

A few years ago I had the opportunity to accompany a group of young people to a refugee camp in Greece. We were there for a week, bringing some awareness and funds to the camp, and trying to help with the day-to-day operations.

While there, I met hundreds of people who were running away from war, and people who had to liquidate everything they ever owned so they could pay smugglers to take them to a safe place. During the journey from Syria or Afghanistan, they were often asked to walk for many days, among the trail of dead bodies of those who did not make it.

Once they reached the sea, they were asked to get on boats—boats that were meant for five people but that would hold up to thirty. They were asked to take off all of their clothes, because when clothes get wet, they get heavy, and the boat can sink as a result. Since it was the middle of winter some of them would simply freeze to death. Men, women, and children. Their dead bodies were then thrown into the sea.

When they were finally about to reach the destination, when, from a distance, they were able to see the shore, they described how there was a moment of feeling relief and joy. They had made it, and their journey was a success! Until, a moment later, they were told, at gunpoint, to jump into the cold water and swim to the shore, even those who didn't know how to swim. Many of them died. Only some made it.

Remembering being there in that camp and being surrounded by those stories, feeling into all the heartbreak while also witnessing all the generosity present and the people who had literally lost everything and were still refusing to give up, bring me to today.

Many of us are still doing okay and have only been touched by the pandemic in relatively minor ways, but this is not the case for many of our neighbors. It is true that no one is literally being asked, at gunpoint, to jump into the sea, but based on the stories we hear from other corners of the world and the long lines we are seeing at soup kitchens and food pantries in a lot of our cities, many of our neighbors feel exactly like they are staring down the barrel of a gun, not sure if they and their families will make it.

It has been said that Covid-19 has been a great equalizer, demonstrating how interconnected we all are, for the virus does not discriminate who gets it. While true on some level, the pandemic has also highlighted the usual inequalities, namely, that some of us seem to always make it because we are given preferential access to resources and care, while others, whole groups of people in fact, are given the crumbs to eat from the floor. Covid-19 may be becoming more manageable, at least for some, but what worries me is not just Covid-19 but the underlying pandemic of indifference to the poor that has been quietly infecting our society for some time now.

The Christian spiritual tradition is very clear about how we are to relate to those who are fragile, who have been rejected and forgotten, and who are standing on the bread lines waiting for food. We are to see them as Christ and approach them with the same kind of reverence and willingness to say yes. This identification of Christ with the poor is such that an old Anglo-Catholic saying, often cited in the context of the slum priest movement of the 1920s, tells us that unless we are willing and able to see Christ on the highways and byways of our cities in those who are rejected, homeless, and poor, we have no business talking about meeting him in the Eucharist. Our faith cannot be complete unless we have connected the two. As one theologian said, "The real presence of Christ, which is hidden in the bread and wine, is visibly manifested in his social presence in the poor who are the sign and image of His ongoing passion in the world."[1]

In Jesus's Parable of the Lost Sheep, we meet the Christ who is the good shepherd, who, like the thousands of volunteers who rescued those refugees from the freezing waters of the Mediterranean Sea, is there searching for those who are lost, in need of being wrapped in literal or metaphorical blankets of motherly love. We meet the One who is an open gate, not unlike the gate of that refugee camp, which made the passage to safety and care possible for so many. I love how frankly Matthew's Gospel puts it:

What do you think? If a shepherd has a hundred sheep, and one of them has gone astray, does he not leave the ninety-nine on the mountains and go in search of the one that went astray? And if he finds it, truly I tell you, he rejoices over it more than over the ninety-nine that never went astray. So it is not the will of your Father in heaven that one of these little ones should be lost. (Matthew 18:12–14)

And then there is what we hear in the First Letter of Peter, that we are to "come to Christ," the very foundation of who we are to become and "stay near." We are to stay near "like infants at the breast, drinking deeply of God's pure life-giving care," taking on God's qualities and growing into maturity. This nearness to Christ will transform us into living stones that can be used to build a spiritual home in which those who lack something can be filled. It is nearness to the ones who were rejected, who need to be brought back into the center, who will correct our vision and fill our own lack.

If only that was how it routinely happened in our lives and communities. It doesn't.

Indeed, Christ comes to us not only in prayer, not only in beautiful celebrations like those that we experience in church on the great festivals and holidays, but also in those who are hungry and thirsty for our presence and our love, in those who ask us for help. And, "our attitude toward them, or better, our commitment to them decides whether our existence is confirmed to the will of God or not."[2] They both open the door to God's house for us and they give us a chance to become the door for others.

We're going to continue to live with this pandemic for months and years, and this pandemic will forever change many important aspects of our lives. We have already become more isolated from one another. We have already exacerbated some of those negative tendencies that were there before the virus and are now growing in us like yet another virus.

I hope that every one of us reflects in prayer as to how we are called to show up in this crisis—and in the next one. Right now many of us may still be preoccupied with how to organize our own lives, given all that has changed in the last few years and the continuous uncertainty. But we still have to find the strength and space to act. If the predictions are correct, it may not be the coronavirus that kills us but hunger. While the health crisis is stabilizing—at least in our small corner of the planet—this may be just the beginning of the crisis that is to follow. Experts tell us that the world has never faced a hunger emergency like the one that is coming as a result of both the coronavirus and climate change.

Where will we be when that happens? How will we show up? Will we be an open gate, like Christ, or a closed gate? I want to believe that we will chase after the sheep who are lost. And will the spiritual home that we are invited to build together with God, and in which people's needs can be held in Christ's transforming care, be ready? What part will you play in what is to come?

CHAPTER 13

Horrors of the Pre- and Postpandemic Normal

"So here we are getting back to normal," a friend said to me on the phone once the restrictions of shelter-in-place were removed, "and I am excited but also already overwhelmed. I want some things to come back but not all things. All tragedies aside," she continued, "last year also brought a lot of gifts. Among them a gift of quiet."

My friend is not alone in naming this—how despite all the tragedies that the pandemic brought to us there were also some unexpected blessings. In fact, research tells us that roughly 90 percent of people in the United States said the pandemic "helped them to reflect on what really matters in life." People talked about finally having time to spend with their loved ones. Climate scientists observed that a month into the quarantine the air in places like Los Angeles became almost crystal clear. The pandemic also led to people spending more time outside, for instance, by going for walks, even visiting national parks in record numbers.

Now that things pretty much have gone back to normal and most businesses are trying to function pretending that the pandemic never happened, so many of us feel relieved that we managed to get a vaccine that prevents serious illness, and at the same time we also feel anxious about whether our nervous systems can actually handle the way life used to be before it all happened. After all, how normal was our way of life before the pandemic? Do we want to go back to how we were? We were living in unsustainable ways, tolerating intolerable inequities. There was not that much normal about our pre-Covid world. We talk about "normal" as a way of coping with the ways things are, or our feeling unable to change them. Wouldn't it be good, once and for all, with this reset afforded us, to do things differently?

Derek Walcott, the Saint Lucian poet and playwright, tells us that "we must fall in love with the world in spite of history."[1] History is full of tragedies. History, at times, has a way of making us feel like we are being pushed against the wall. History hurts and makes people tired. But, as the poet said, we must fall in love with the world in spite of all that. Elaborating on this, theologian Matthew Fox writes that "especially when history becomes ugly and mean, we have to dig deep into the 'ground of our being' and rejuvenate our passion for living, our passion for beauty, in order to stay grounded, be strong and commit to birthing a new future."[2]

How do we do this? How do we fall in love with the world in spite of all the tragedies? How do we get to that place where we feel our passion rejuvenated? Our passion for living? Our passion for beauty? Our passion for saying no to protect our time and our souls from all the meaningless distractions that tend to confuse us? How do we get out of the stuckness we so often feel, out of this darkness? How do we convert what sometimes feels like a tomb into a womb where new creation and new birthing can happen?

Saint Paul tells us that this can happen by touching Christ. What intriguing imagery and language this is! The Christian mystical tradition offers this strange way of accessing God. "If anyone is in Christ," he says, "there is a new creation" (2 Corinthians 5:17). *In* Christ, *touching* Christ, *with* Christ, we are rejuvenated. This is why ancient Christians often talked of baptism as spiritual regeneration and rebirth. Not just a bath, not only a symbol.

During the initial year of the pandemic, almost as if by chance, through tragedy and mandatory withdrawal from life as we knew it, many of us touched that deep ground of our being. Many of us touched that deep space within and were able to get a glimpse of the kind of normal we didn't even know we longed for. What might it be? Not our usual normal, but a more kind and humane normal, a quieter and gentler world, a normal worth fighting for!

This is where the teachings of Jesus come in. In three parables of Jesus, we hear and see him talking about seeds and the earth. This is important. We have the Parable of the Sower, the Parable of the Growing Seed, and the Parable of the Mustard Seed (Matthew 13:1–23; Mark 4:26–29; and Mark 4:30–32). Consider simply the way that Jesus's mind and imagination work. Where does he look for examples of how we ought to live? This tells us that by paying attention to the earth we are paying attention to God. God's revelation, as St. Thomas Aquinas told us a long time ago, "Comes in two volumes: the Bible and nature."

Matthew Fox, in his classic book on creation-centered spirituality, *Original Blessing*, tells us that in a culture such as ours, saturated with words, we have to remember that "the human word is only one among billions of words that God has spoken." And to make contact with wisdom, to touch our real ground, to drink from that inner spring of life, Fox says sometimes it is helpful "to go beyond human words, which have, after all, existed for only about four million years—and have appeared in print for only five hundred years."[3] It is helpful to go beyond our cognitive ways of receiving information and instead listen to the earth. Not just with our ears but also with our hearts and our whole bodies. Creation, after all, speaks with a language that is much older than human words and stores within itself four and a half billion years of wise advice from God. Another biblical scholar says, "Creation not only exists, it also discharges truth."[4] It helps us to connect with the Christ present at the heart of all that exists, and be renewed.

So this is my hope: that before we forget about all the insights we have had about our lives during the time of mandatory withdrawal and move on into our usual normal we make sure we don't waste the lessons we have learned. Let's make sure that we do not waste this opportunity to create a new normal for our lives and our world. I am beginning to make a list for myself. I am hearing my friends with their own lists and desires. I think a new normal is possible, but only if we get up off the couch of the false allure of the way things were.

Listen for the voice of God in your midst. I would sit there with you, now, to listen together with you, if I could. Listen to God's advice in the wind and the rain. I will do the same. Hear how it is there to help you stay strong, to help you resist going back to the frantic world you once knew. And, instead, make choices that will be good for all of us and for the world.

PART THREE

Interrupting Silence

CHAPTER 14

"I Refuse to Go to a Homophobic Heaven"

His name was Mali; he loved impersonating Lady Gaga, and he was quite good at it. I met him at a local youth center where I occasionally led a contemplative prayer group. Once he got to know me, he asked me to accompany him to a meeting with his family. "It is time," he said, "that they hear and accept me for who I am." He said he wanted me to witness it. I was hoping to do that.

Mali came from a very devout religious family, but it was a family in which there was no room for boys like him, who didn't conform to what the preacher said was the right way of being a boy. Being in that family, unseen and unreceived, felt suffocating to Mali. He had really tried to be a good son, to be what they wanted, but something within told him that it was better to be free, to be who God created him to be, rather than miss life pretending to be someone else.

So he invited me along to bear witness and to be part of the conversation with his mom and his sister.

I remember meeting and talking with them as if it were yesterday. His family was lovely really, except when he talked to them about being gay. And when he did, it's not like they changed and got nasty. They just simply ignored that part of the conversation. It was almost as if he all of a sudden transitioned into a language that they could not understand. So he would talk, and they would just stare into space. Then when it came time for them to respond they would simply say to me, ignoring what Mali just said and ignoring him, how special Mali was, how much they loved him, and how one day he would find a beautiful girl with whom he would fall in love and have beautiful children.

It took a lot of energy to help them hear what they needed to hear that day, and when they finally did, the anger in the room was palpable. His mom actually said, "You know, your dad had a feeling about you when you were just a child. You were always very feminine. He was afraid that you would turn out to be exactly how you turned out. I wish we had killed, strangled you then so we would not have to deal with you now." You probably shudder to read these words, now. Imagine how they hit Mali as his own mother threw them at him.

As you can imagine, it is very hard to reach any kind of understanding once something like that is said. Mali really tried, but how do you ever come back from that? How do you ever trust again? And it is not that his family was bad. It's just that they didn't know any better. "Being gay is a sin," is what their preacher always told them. And yet, when their child came out to them, they committed the biggest sin of all, because what else do you call it when we cast our children out of our hearts?

In my years of accompanying LGBTQ young people

struggling with homelessness, religious parents expressing a desire to kill their children upon learning about their
sexual orientation was an all-too-common story. Indeed,
there are many churches today that preach that homosexu-
ality is a sin, a condition worse than death. It is not sur-
prising, therefore, that to many observers, being religious—
and especially Christian—today seems synonymous with
being homophobic, bigoted, closeminded—also, by the way,
nationalistic, pro-gun, and obsessed with wealth.

It is therefore our duty to take a stand on behalf of God's
loved ones and welcome all of our LGBTQ siblings, whoever
they love. It is important to say out loud for all to hear: We
celebrate you. We love you. We receive you. You are a gift
to our community. It is important to beg for the forgiveness of our churches' sins, knowing that our LGBTQ siblings, too, are the church. Whoever has rejected them has
excluded themselves from the fellowship that is Christ. It is
important to stand with Archbishop Desmond Tutu, one of
the spiritual giants of our tradition, who said, "I refuse to
worship a God who is homophobic or go to a homophobic
heaven when I die. If I am taken to a homophobic heaven,
I will say, I am sorry, I would much rather go to that other
place."

For many people, this means they need to let go of what
they thought they knew so clearly. I know how difficult that
is. We so often hold our beliefs close-fisted and refuse to
budge on them as a way of holding the world in place and
knowing where we stand in it. But that rarely works, and
it causes a lot of suffering. Change is inventible, and our

understanding of the sacred is deepening and evolving. We need to seek God's presence in actual life circumstances and not our frozen image of them.

Jesus insisted on lives of change, flexibility, and openness to the unknown. I am reminded of a very dramatic passage from the Gospel of Mark. In it, a young rich man asks Jesus for a word of advice on how to begin moving toward holiness and how to inherit eternal life. We are told that Jesus looked the young man in the eye with love, acknowledging his sincerity and years of spiritual practice, and said, "There's one thing left for you to do to inherit eternal life: Go sell whatever you own and give it to the poor. All your wealth will then be heavenly wealth. And when you do that, come follow me."

According to the Gospel, the young man's face clouded over, and he walked away with a heavy heart. This was the last thing he expected to hear. He was not ready to let go of what he owned, the very things that gave him a sense of stability and protection from the unstable world.

What a dramatic and sad encounter!

Some years ago, I read about a research study on the consequences of having or owning too much. In this research, two Berkeley psychologists designed their study based on the following question: "Who is more likely to lie, cheat, and steal—the poor person or the rich one?" "It's tempting to think that the wealthier you are, the more likely you are to act fairly," they said. "After all, if you already have enough for yourself, it's easier to think about what others may need." But in their research they discovered the exact opposite to be true. "As people climb the social ladder, their compassionate feelings toward other people decline." The researchers suspected that the reason for this "may have something to do with how wealth and abundance give us a sense of freedom and independence from others. The less we have to rely on others, the less we may care about their feelings. This leads us toward being more self-focused."[1]

This, I believe, may be the heart of the message. To let go of the stuff of our lives, be it money, privilege, our beliefs, or whatever else that prompts us to feel that it is acceptable to put people out of our hearts and simply walk away. To let go of the idea that spirituality is about what we do with our individual lives, or even how best to shelter our lives from "unwanted influences." To let go of any illusions we harbor that the spiritual life is about anything other than learning to travel and struggle and love and depend on one another, together, no matter how messy it gets.

The kind of spirituality Jesus calls us to is less about withdrawal, protection, safety, and preserving our lives as we know them, and more about risk, vulnerability, and even mutual dependence. On this path, we make progress not by practicing "shelter in place" but by being able to touch what frightens us in the world. We make progress by removing the protective walls, the clear boundaries dividing the world into good and bad, and engaging with it, struggling with it, and in the process, discovering new levels of God's expansiveness.

On this path, we are asked to let go of what prompts us to reject people even before considering their experience and, instead, touch what is foreign to us. We touch what is foreign to us so that we may risk being changed by it, because we know there is no transformation without change. This is what conversion—a lifelong process—is all about. As my friend Fr. Michael Holleran once said to me, if you have not changed your mind on any of the big issues you believe in, most likely you have not been following the guidance of the Holy Spirit in your life. Most likely you have not been open enough to people to hear what God may be whispering to you through them. The lesson that Jesus is teaching seems to be that simple.

May we all learn how to stop creating boundaries that protect us from what is inconvenient or unknown. May we no longer be stuck by a fear of becoming tainted by others or the world, but instead commit to being in relationship with what we normally want to reject. So that we can discover a deeper perspective. So that we can discover that what we fear outside in the world we most likely also fear in ourselves. So we can know that there is no holiness without wholeness, in us and in our community. Salvation is a group activity and our destiny depends on our ability to struggle through things together.

CHAPTER 15

Praying with the Street Church of Radical Forgiveness

Each year when we commemorate the anniversary of 9/11, I remember well all the images of that day. The horror and devastation are still very present with me, even now. I also remember that in the days following the tragedy, here in New York, glimmers of hope and resilience began to emerge. People spontaneously began gathering in public places, like Union Square in Manhattan, to commence impromptu public grieving ceremonies. There were Buddhist monks praying for compassion. There was Rev. Billy, an actor fashioning himself as a priest of the church of radical forgiveness, offering absolutions to anyone who was willing to confess their sins. There were young Muslim activists correcting inaccurate portrayals of Islam by our media and proclaiming Islam as a religion of peace. All of a sudden there seemed to be enough money to care for the poor. If you looked unwell, strangers would come up to you on the NYC subway and make sure that you were all right.

Grief softened our hearts, and pain made us aware of other people's suffering. There was a certain holiness in the air during those days. We were seeing with new eyes and hearing with new ears.

But then, about two weeks after the tragedy, we were told that everything needed to go back to normal. Memorials were cleared out of public spaces. Public prayers were discouraged. To be normal, we were told, was to go shopping because that was good for our country. To be normal, we were told, was to cease congregating in public places.

We were told to go back to normal and that we did. It's just that normal was not really normal to begin with.

Around that time, a friend invited me to a Bible study, without providing too many details. I simply knew that it was located on the Upper West Side at a community house of Jesuit priests. The class was led by an elderly man named Dan. He seemed like a very kind and gentle man. His voice was soft, and his insight into the text quite profound. It felt like he lived the text we were studying. It was only afterward that I discovered that this man "Dan" was the famous Jesuit priest Daniel Berrigan, who had spent his life protesting the values of American society that he felt contradicted the gospel of the nonviolent Jesus. His protests included hundreds of acts of civil disobedience, an illegal trip to Vietnam in the midst of the American invasion of Vietnam, and even time in hiding during which he topped the FBI's Most Wanted list.

I met Dan a couple more times after that first encounter. He was invited to preach at a post 9/11 wedding of a friend at a Polish Catholic Church in Brooklyn. I'll never forget the confused facial expression of the very traditional Polish priest who was officiating the wedding when he realized that Dan was preaching a sermon about the then-recent American invasion of Iraq. The Polish priest's eyes were screaming, "This is a wedding! You should be preaching about love!" But, you see, in Dan's mind he *was* preaching about love. Because for him love was not love unless it completely transformed us and changed how we live, what we say yes and no to, and how we let Christ live, love, work, and protest through us. Also, since in the Christian tradition marriage is supposed to be an earthly analogy for union with God, the kind of love that needs to be preached at a wedding is a love that is not small and fluffy but a love that's got edges and is willing to suffer bruises in its commitment to embody what Christ stood for in the world. (Dan didn't explain that in his sermon, and I never said any of that to the Polish priest, but perhaps I should have!)

In Matthew 18, we are presented with an illustration that takes place after a full day of ministry, following Jesus's instructions to the disciples about being good shepherds. The disciples have been quarrelling about how many chances they should give to people who keep on missing the mark and making mistakes, even the same mistakes. How many times should we forgive those who harm us? Given that, in the first century, the typical rabbinic standard was to forgive up to three times, Peter might have thought his suggestion to forgive seven times was generous. Jesus's response, however, was shocking. He said that we shouldn't just forgive three or four or even seven times. We should forgive seventy-seven times, and there really should be no limit to our forgiveness.

Commenting on the importance of this limitless forgiveness, another great teacher, Henri Nouwen, said:

> To forgive another person from the heart is an act of liberation. We set that person free from the negative bonds that exist between us. We say, "I no longer hold your offense against you." But there is more. We also free ourselves from the burden of being the "offended one." As long as we do not forgive those who have wounded us, we carry them with us or, worse, pull them as a heavy load. The great temptation is to cling in anger to our enemies and then define ourselves as being offended and wounded by them. Forgiveness, therefore, liberates not only the other but also us. It is the way to the freedom of the children of God.[1]

Forgiveness doesn't have to mean forgetfulness. To forgive is to cancel the expectation of payment for the offense and to be free from any attempt to "get even." To forgive is to choose not to carry the burden with us anymore and to be open to the freshness of a new start. Forgiveness opens up possibilities for healing, reconciliation, and mercy—but not just mercy, also justice, the kind of justice that seeks not to punish but to heal.

Speaking of the freedom that forgiveness offers, I am reminded of one of the thousands of stories of perpetrators and survivors of the Rwandan genocide who took refuge in the practice of forgiveness that Jesus proposed. Jean Claude was a young eleven-year-old in Rwanda when the genocide began there. Tragically, as he hid in the bushes, he watched as neighbors tortured, mutilated, and murdered his father, sister, aunts, and uncles. After the genocide, Jean Claude wondered how to move on and eventually made the choice to forgive those who had murdered his family. Years later, he started a nonprofit to help poor and orphaned children. Most of the children that his organization supported came from the families that committed the genocide. When asked about his choice to support orphaned children of those who committed all the atrocities he said,

> If I could not have forgiven, I would have said that I can only help the genocide survivors. But then I would not be able to help this one child that I now love so much. He is a child of a man who participated in the killing of my father. After the genocide when his father was imprisoned for his crimes, I knew that this child needed help. I decided to adopt him. I knew what it felt like to lose a father and I didn't want him to have the same experience that I did. So I took him in and now am raising him as my own son.[2]

This is what forgiveness in action looks like and this is how the gospel is lived in real life.

So now I return in my memory to the aftermath of 9/11, and I imagine what might have happened if the screams of pundits who occupied our media, many of whose voices are still present today, had been replaced by the voices of people like Jean Claude, willing to do the hard work of putting forgiveness in action. How would these intervening years have been different if restorative justice had been our guiding principle? Imagine if on September 12th, instead of rushing into the logic of retaliation and war, we had taken a pause to fast, and to pray, and to deeply listen to the grievances of those who had been hurt as a result of our policies and presence? Just imagine how different our lives and our politics would be today.

We can't go back and fix all the mistakes of the past, but we can move forward by going *inward*, searching our hearts for those hard areas in need of the giving and receiving of forgiveness, praying "Abba . . . Father, forgive us our trespasses, as we forgive those who trespass against us."

CHAPTER 16

Field Hospitals for Those Wounded by Life

It was in autumn of 2002 and I was in India. I was a resident of a community located in the slums about twenty kilometers outside Delhi. I spent just a few months there, but what I experienced changed my life and marked a real beginning of my vocation.

The community was a home to many people who were rescued from the streets. On the first day of my stay, I remember seeing a boy who was brought to us. He was a young teenager, his body, face, and head were all swollen and looked like an open wound. We were told that he had been beaten with a stick by an adult who was frustrated by the boy's inability to express himself and follow instructions. As it turned out, the boy was mentally disabled. I will never forget seeing him for the first time: he was in a state of complete shock, screaming, running, crying. It took so much to calm him down.

Our whole community was built of people like this boy. Looking back, I remember well some of the faces of our residents. There was also Suresh, a young Nepalese boy missing a limb because someone threw him out of a moving train. There was Radha, a little girl found in the arms of her dead mother who overdosed on heroine. There was Mohamed, who when he was no longer useful to his adult son because of his advanced age, was thrown out on the street and asked to look for a new life. Our community was full of stories like that. Tragic stories. But also stories of great perseverance and hope. And we all had a chance to become a family again. All of a sudden an elder thrown out on the street had a chance to become a grandfather figure to an abandoned street kid. In our community each day we were learning how to give and receive love. We met Christ that way; he was the love that we generated, and the love that made our lives bearable and even good again.

Then a day came when we were told that one of our sponsoring churches from the United States would be visiting to see how we were using the funds they had been sending. We were told that they had been supporting us with funds and prayer for some time now and that they were eager to experience our community firsthand.

When they arrived, we invited them to pray and live with us. They were able to see that in our community hundreds of people, who really should have been dead considering their circumstances, were somehow resurrected back to life. They saw all of that. They tasted the love that was present among us. But, somehow, it was not enough. What they wanted to hear, what was most important to them, was to know how many of our residents had accepted Jesus as their personal lord and savior. When I heard their question, it took me only a moment to respond. The answer was easy. "None of our residents have accepted Jesus as their personal savior because that is not our focus."

Knowing the history of India, knowing the history of colonialism, knowing that most of our residents were Hindu or Muslim, and knowing what Christian missionaries had done to their country, their culture, and their ancestors, we considered it more important for us to be Christ for others rather than to argue or bully people into some kind of artificial change of religion so that we could feel justified in loving them. The last thing our community wanted to do was what we saw some Christian ministries do: Using service as a means to get people to convert, and demanding that people convert just so they could be recipients of basic services like food and shelter. Besides, living in India, we saw how so many of our Hindu, Sufi, and Buddhist friends had a much more profound insight into the reality of God and Christ than the Christians we knew. And it was not only what they were able to articulate. It is what they lived.

So, yes, Jesus was there with us in our community. Like holy incense, Christ's presence was undeniable, but not always named. His love simply was. It was made manifest in simple acts of presence and care.

But that wasn't enough for our visitors. Seeing people resurrected back to life was not enough. They wanted more. Or, at least, something else.

Their visit, as you can imagine, did not end well. In fact, after staying with us for a couple of days, they even wrote an open letter to other churches supporting our ministry in an attempt to block other funding we were receiving. Why? Because we were not producing new churchgoers. Because we were not conquering what they considered to be a "godless country" to their very uniquely and decidedly American version of Jesus they so desperately wanted to incarnate everywhere they went.

In Mark 7, we are presented with a story of a Syro-Phoenician woman, and the story goes like this: Jesus ventures into non-Jewish territory, where he is trying to keep a low profile, but in the process he is approached by a non-Jewish woman who begs him for help. Her little girl is not well; and so she finds Jesus, sits at his feet, and begs him to heal her girl.

First of all, by approaching Jesus, the woman is breaking all religious and cultural norms: as a Gentile (not Jewish) she is considered impure. Also, she is a woman, and the rules then about how and when a woman might approach a man were, as you might imagine, very different from today.

Jesus's initial response is shocking, to say the least. He says "It is not good to take the bread of the children and throw it to the dogs." Even after Jesus experiences his God as an expansive and loving parent, and even after accusing some of the religious leaders of his day of being mere play-actors paying too much attention to human laws and failing to grasp the transformative power of God, Jesus's words to this woman seem to reveal the ingrained exclusivity and maybe even prejudice and xenophobia of the culture present in him. Reacting to this, the woman says "Lord: even the dogs under the table eat from the scraps of the children."[1]

This does something to Jesus. This awakens something in him. This makes him stop and see what perhaps he had not seen before. This, as St. John Chrysostom tells us in the fifth century in his commentary on this passage, awakens his compassion. This enables Jesus to embody compassion in his response. He tells her that, because of her response, her daughter is now healed. The woman returns home to find that this is true.

The meaning of compassion in Jesus's language and culture is derived from the name of the most motherly organ a human can possess—the womb. Jesus's experience with the Syro-Phoenician woman possibly expands his understanding of his own vocation, from serving as the Messiah, the son of David, whose mission was to focus on his own Jewish people, letting them know that their long-awaited search for liberation was at hand, to also embracing his wider role as a universal instrument of God's healing and salvation for all.[2]

We all need to follow the journey Jesus took—a path that can awaken our hearts and enable us to see our mission with new eyes—or else we will keep on destroying God's work like those well-meaning but misguided Christians did when they came to visit our community in India. We need to be willing to be present to the circumstances of our world and be changed by them. On the one hand, we need to continue our traditions and our ways of initiating people into the experience of God in Christ; we need to continue to minister to our own. On the other hand, especially with the church shrinking, as it is, we need to understand that God may be doing something new, and that God's mission, our mission, needs to be bigger than the church or making new Christians.

Listening to church leaders, I am often struck by how detached from reality we really are. We interpret our reality primarily through an assumption that young people are not interested in the sacred and that making new Christians and building up the institution is the only metric worth focusing on.

It is true that the number of churchgoers is shrinking, and young people in particular are leaving. We have fewer baptisms each year and fewer church weddings. It is also true that we have all kinds of stories to explain this mass exodus. We even come up with catchy phrases such as "moralistic therapeutic deism" to explain why the numbers are getting smaller and smaller. Most of our stories and explanations tend to point to the deficiencies of the people who leave and to an increasingly hostile climate toward religion in our contemporary world. But we should remember that we are mostly facing a situation of our own making. One thing that is clear to anyone who is listening is that young people are leaving our churches not because they are no longer interested in lives of meaning, purpose, and significance, and not because they are no longer interested in God. They are leaving because, from where they are standing, it is increasingly difficult to meet God in the church.

Young people (and let's think of the Syro-Phoenician woman as one of them) tell us that, even if we do have a corner on the truth, the church resembles—in too many ways—every other broken system that organizes around power, wealth, and privilege rather than offering itself as a radical alternative to the status quo. This generation is telling us that Christ has left the building and the tabernacle is empty, that it is easier to meet Christ elsewhere. This dramatic change is reflected in new studies on the religious landscape of America, which tell us that while Millennials and Generation Z show the lowest level of religious affiliation compared to previous generations, they also show the highest level of desire for spiritual connection. In popular culture, we call this the "spiritual but not religious" or "the nones" phenomenon. Many people also choose to embrace "dual belonging" or a more interspiritual path. It is not that they are not interested in the sacred; they are simply not interested in religion that is stale, spiritually bankrupt, and no longer able to speak to and address some of the big questions of our time.

When millions are starving, when Black kids are being executed on the streets of our cities by the same people who should be protecting them, when Mother Earth is crying as we go on with "business as usual," refusing to address our damaging addictions to comfort and consumerism, it is time for us to wake up, take stock of who we are, acknowledge the resources we have, expand our understanding of our vocation as Christians, and put our spiritual and material resources to better use.

We need to show up on the streets of our cities and offer what we have without asking for a religious compliance test. We need to be there for people in such a way that our words and actions may become a mirror in which they can see who they really are in God. Our buildings, literally and symbolically, need to become, as Pope Francis said, "field hospitals," where those wounded by the battles of this life can come in and receive care. We need to give and give, trusting that it is not self-preservation and endless growth but rather self-spending that lies at the heart of our call. Most of all, we need to remember that God's mission is bigger than we think and that God is already at work in many places where the church is not. "God," after all, as one of our elders, Desmond Tutu, reminded us, "is not a Christian."

So look for the presence of God around you, be open to being surprised by what you see, and then do your best to nourish its emergence in your midst. The future of the world depends on all of our ability to awaken and grow our hearts.

CHAPTER 17

When One Homeless Kid Found His Calling

If you are somewhat familiar with the sayings of Jesus from the New Testament Gospels, you have likely heard this one. What do you think when you hear these familiar words, "Then Jesus told his disciples, 'If any want to become my followers, let them deny themselves and take up their cross and follow me. For those who want to save their life will lose it, and those who lose their life for my sake will find it'" (Matthew 16:24–25)?

These are not easy words. They remind me of a difficult decision I must make all the time. A decision to step out of the driver's seat of my life and become less, so that God can become more. What does that look like? When I think of this process of personal divestment that mystics sometimes call "dying to self," the story comes to mind that shows me what the process may look like in my everyday life.

Some years ago, I met a young person who approached me for some advice. He had just turned twenty-one and wanted to discern how he wanted to spend his life, and who he wanted to become. His story was unique. He had spent the first few years of life in a very loving home, but then in his early teens, after his mom died, ended up in a group home and eventually in a homeless shelter. But he was one of those really bright kids who made every room he entered shine. There was this presence that accompanied him and made people around him feel better.

But what I initially did not know about him was that he also carried a great burden within and that this light that everyone saw came at a great price. Something that very few people knew was that he was born with HIV. He himself did not know for a long time until one day a family member sat him down to explain how he was different from other kids. When he found out, he became extremely frightened, as those were the days of great fear of HIV. It took him a long time to come to terms with what was his to carry in this life, especially since his mom had died of HIV/AIDS, which frightened him even more about what his future held in store. One of the ways he dealt with all of this was to keep it a secret and not tell a living soul. It was almost as if not telling anyone about his HIV made the fact that he had it not really real.

So, I was surprised when he approached me to talk about his future, and when he said that he would like me to help him discern as to whether he should start speaking publicly about his HIV status. He said he had already been mentoring kids who were diagnosed with HIV, and now there was an opportunity available to him to become a public spokesperson for a big awareness-and-prevention campaign. But becoming part of this campaign would mean going public with his status.

We talked and prayed about it for some time, but deep within my heart I had concerns. My biggest concern was that once his peers knew about this secret he had held so tightly for so many years, his life would change drastically. They may begin to treat him differently. So we talked for a long time. Ultimately, unable to reach a clear decision as to what he should do, we agreed that we would take some more time to pray about this before talking again.

After that, I didn't see him for many weeks, until one day unexpectedly he came back saying that he was ready to talk again. He said that he had made his decision and wanted to go public with his status and become a spokesperson and a mentor in the HIV-awareness campaign. When I heard this, I resisted, again, frightened for how his life would change. Wanting to push against his wish I asked, "But why? Why do you want to do this?" And I will never forget what he said to me.

Looking at me with a seriousness that I had not seen before in him, he said:

> I want to do this because every time I speak to young people with HIV, every time I share the pain and the hope that I have for myself and for them, every time I mentor someone newly diagnosed, I feel as if there is an angel sitting on my shoulders. And it is in those moments that I know that this is why I was born. I was born to do this very thing. To be the presence of support for those who are frightened, for those who have no hope. And now, I want to be that and embody

that more fully and be a sign of life for those who feel that their lives are being taken away from them. This is why I want to do this. And the fact that my friends may start treating me differently once they know that I have HIV is a risk that I am willing to take. This is my burden to carry. And carrying it without fighting with it gives me great freedom. A freedom that enables me to show up for others in a new way and with a new hope. Today, I know that I no longer have to apologize for who I am. Today, I know that I have a purpose, and it is bigger than what the world tells me my life can be.

I was convinced. How could I not be!? Here, I was supposedly mentoring this kid and giving him advice, when in fact, it was I who was being mentored by his great insight and wisdom. It was I who was given a gift of seeing how saying yes to our crosses freely and openly can take us into a new life.

So this takes me back to Jesus's statement about taking up our cross and following him, with all that that entails. What does it mean to deny myself as I take up that cross—and what is that cross?—and step into this mysterious power that Christ is?

I think, first, I can learn that to deny myself means to deny the world's hold on how and who I should be. Because while all the programs for happiness that our books and podcasts initiate us into promise us perks like relevance, belonging, happiness, and success, they say very little to us about the will of God and what true aliveness in God looks and feels like. Letting go of all that will not be pleasant, and it will often feel like a certain kind of death. But in this life, there are many deaths that I have to experience before I reach my actual physical death. And those deaths are my only sure passage into heavenly, divine life.

I think, second, I can learn that to take up my cross means to come to terms with the fact that while this life is full of unfair circumstances, unavoidable suffering, and frustration, I ought to do everything I can to come to peace with the fact that even in my most challenging circumstances great gifts can be found. Accepting this helps me to stay open and be surprised by how God may show up. Bitterness, on the other hand, blocks my vision of all the goodness that surrounds me. Bitterness separates me from God and makes me deaf to God's voice.

And finally, when I recall how long it took this young man to make the right decision, I think I can learn that following God is often accompanied by long periods of what feels like meaningless and confusing waiting during which I have to face my own demons and temptations, the biggest of all being the temptation to quit. It is so easy to quit, to say, I'm not up to this, or, it won't be good for me. It's often temptation—may I even say the tempter?—that speaks these things into my mind and heart. But as Ronald Rolheiser has said, in this life, "all symphonies must remain unfinished";[1] and "sometimes in the midst of pain the best we can do is to put our mouths to the dust and wait. . . . Wait . . . in frustration, wait inside injustice, inside pain, wait in longing."[2]

This waiting is never in vain. This waiting is never without promise. Because when I least expect it there does come a time when Christ's light breaks into my midst, and I am able to glimpse what all of this is about. The veil is lifted, even if just for a moment, and what I had seen from a distance and mistaken for an unclear, moving shape, reveals itself to be a person with a face and voice. A voice that is calling my name. A voice that tells me that all this was to prepare me to become like clay that can be shaped into a special vessel for taking God's goodness into the world.

When that happens, with St. Symeon the New Theologian I may be able to say, "We awaken in Christ's body just as Christ awakens our bodies." And with St. Paul, I can say that now, "It is no longer I who live, but it is Christ who lives in me."[3] And like the young man I talked about, I may taste the true freedom that only surrender to a power greater than ourselves can bring. I will become a bridge, a lamp, and a sanctuary for those who have lost their way and are in need of hope.

CHAPTER 18

Claiming Our Irrelevance
So God Can Be Relevant

There is a place in the Gospels where people who are impressed by some of Jesus's signs and healings begin to follow him, even as he travels into a pretty remote place. Seeing this mass of people and anticipating that the crowd will soon grow hungry, Jesus decides it is a perfect moment to teach his disciples a lesson. He asks "Where can we buy some food to feed all these people?"

Clearly not catching his point, one disciple throws up his hands in despair, saying that it would take a fortune to buy enough food to feed the crowd. Then another disciple rather sheepishly says something like, "Hey, there's a kid here with some lunch." Maybe that disciple had reached the point of desperation. And perhaps the boy thought it was a joke. "There's no way my little lunch can feed a crowd!"

But Jesus takes the suggestion seriously and tells the disciples to instruct the people to sit down and prepare for a meal. Then Jesus takes the boy's five loaves of barely bread and two fish, says a blessing over the food, and then the food is distributed to the people. When all is said and done, there are twelve baskets of leftovers; and everyone feels satisfied. (See John 6:1–14.) Wow! What a story!

What strikes me most, at this point in my life, is the helplessness that the disciples seem to feel when faced with a question about feeding all the people present. It is an important ingredient in this account. The disciples feel inadequate to respond to the need. They see the need and then contemplate a list of things needed before they can begin to address it. They wonder about money and where to buy the goods.

But Jesus proposes a different solution. Instead of going outside, he suggests going inside, into themselves and into the group. What is it that we already have? What is it that those whom we normally dismiss as irrelevant among us, like a young boy with just a little bit of food, have? This is the material needed for addressing the world's needs. Not some imaginary situation in which we have access to unlimited resources, as nice as that may be, but rather what we already possess and who we already are. Jesus calls us just as we are, not as we wish to be. You are enough. I am enough. Jesus calls us just as we are and takes care of the rest, provided we let him. Now, that, I suggest, is quite a story!

But what we have is enough only if we can entrust it to Christ and let him turn it into something usable. This implies a partnership. This implies that we have to claim all we have and all we are, even if we find it very unimpressive, and then entrust it to him, saying, "Here is my offering. Take it. Use it. Transform it. Make it beautiful."

At the risk of sounding like a priest, this is so eucharistic. If you are Christian and you still attend church of some kind, think about this. We gather together and bring the stuff of our lives. We bring our gifts and place them in the offering basket. We also bring all of those things that may remain unnamed: fears, worries, mortality, even sickness. We bring our dreams and also our wounds. We place all of that on a table and ask Christ to take it. To change it and make it usable. To transform it into something that can reflect his life, his wholeness, his hope. Then, once the prayers are said over the bread and wine, bread and wine that symbolize all of our named and unnamed offerings, we receive it back again, transformed. We receive it as something that can infuse us with his very life. So, what's broken in us can be restored. What's not enough can become enough. Our wounds and fears can be transformed into gifts—gifts we can offer the world. So those who are hungry can be fed. So those who are suffering can get better.

When I think of this Gospel passage, I often think of my time of working with homeless youth. I spent years building skills and learning tools and, in the process, felt that I would become a capable professional armed with therapeutic skills and techniques that could fix people's lives. Deep down, I really believed that I was there among the homeless fixing their lives. Until one day I realized that what I was doing was not really working. Kids were going through our programs and still ending up on the street. Kids were going through our programs, and they were still just one step from being hurt or even killed by a drug dealer or pimp. That is when I was forced to change. I started feeling helpless, and my confidence was shattered. All that I was left with was faith. All that I was left with was trust that I was where God was calling me to be.

As a result of the crisis I underwent, my work evolved from a highly praised, solution-oriented, and evidence-based practice into something much more intuitive. It really moved into prayer. And when I say prayer, I don't necessarily mean that I was saying prayers with people. Instead, I started showing up for every person who needed my help in the same way that I was showing up for prayer. Gathering all my knowledge and tools and entrusting them to God. Saying to God, "I think you're calling me to do something here. This is what I come with. I offer it to you. Take it. Change it. Make it useful. Because I feel so small and useless here." I would just be there with homeless youth in a state of not knowing and trust. Paying attention to what was, bearing witness to their pain, helping them to hold their pain, and often breaking with them as a result of what I was witnessing. How could I not break to hear all the stories of abuse they experienced? How could I not break hearing about all the violence and hurt?

And what I began discovering is that every time I allowed myself to feel at a loss in the face of the pain I witnessed, every time I touched my own irrelevance, there was this energy of God that would begin to emerge in our midst. All I had to do was say yes to it. The presence of God was there, always ready to pick up the broken pieces from the floor and re-assemble them into something good, into something wholesome. And when that happened, I realized that my skills were not useless. I just needed to first surrender them to God, so God could use them however God wished. So right words could come. So right ways of being present could manifest. And when that happened, it was often not clear who was helping whom. Because in each of those sacred moments I received just as much as I was giving, if not more.

I think this is how God works. In moments when we take honest stock of our lives and simply surrender who we are and what we have to God, no matter how useless, God becomes the actor who acts through us. God becomes the writer of our lives, and we become a pencil with which God writes a love letter to the world. That is how Mother Teresa used to put it—and she understood it so very well.

This is what is really happening in that story of the feeding of the five thousand. The boy, who is an unlikely candidate to save the day, becomes a vehicle for a sign pointing to God's tremendous generosity and gift. The unimpressive, the not enough, is being blessed and changed and multiplied; and people are fed. They are fed not just with bread and fishes but with God. This is our invitation, too. To become the very material that God can transform into something that can feed the many hungers of our world.

CHAPTER 19

It Is Time to Fast and Pray for the Future

I recently spent a few years living in Wisconsin. When I got there, I decided to get a membership at a local gym. Part of the motivation was to be able to exercise but also to watch the news, since I didn't have a TV at home.

I love watching the news while exercising on the treadmill, and gyms are very good at having all the cable news channels. So you can get two things for the price of one. Get a gym membership and have access to cable news! As someone who grew up under a totalitarian regime where news was tightly controlled and censored by the government, I enjoy having access to different networks and different points of view. On any given day, I like to look at the progressive, liberal, conservative, and anything in-between news outlets.

At first, my workouts were a success. I got my exercise, and I got my daily dose of the news. Then one day, I got on the treadmill, started my exercise regimen but couldn't find any news channels on the TV screen attached to my machine. So I moved to the next machine, and there, too, no news was to be found. After a few minutes, I decided to pause my workout and go downstairs to talk to the front desk person. After all, watching the news was the more important half of the reason I was there in the first place!

I approached the front desk person and kindly asked why all the news channels had disappeared from my TV. Somewhat apologetically and perplexed, she replied that people were simply too triggered by seeing what news channel their exercise neighbors were watching and that this was leading to arguments and fights. And after a fist fight broke out between two gym-goers, the management decided to ban all the news channels from the facility. Somewhat shocked, I said, "So basically the only way to have peace in this place is to limit people's access to information?" "That's exactly right," the worker replied. "We are here to be a symbol of unity for our community, and we just had too many fights over what people were watching."

Every four years, our country witnesses the inauguration of a president. Most recently, the occasion was accompanied by many beautiful celebrations and speeches, with a very moving poem by twenty-two-year-old National Youth Poet Laureate, Amanda Gorman, stealing the show. As one Black journalist acknowledged that day, while poetry "won't literally pass legislation or deflect a bullet from exploding in my Black body, a poem is what makes our hearts move." And certainly today, more than ever, we need our hearts to be moved and opened.

Four years earlier, after Donald Trump was elected president, Rev. William Barber, the leader of the Poor People's

Campaign, said that the right response to this news was to fast, repent, and pray. Four years later, after the inauguration of someone who was not Donald Trump, I believe we still need the same response. In fact, as Christians, we are always to have this response, because this moves us from relying on and trusting too much in political ideologies and takes us into the possibility of relying on God. Fasting, repenting, and praying help us to stop playing God. It enables us to accept that we are part of the problems we see in the world and approach one another and the difficulties we face with humility. It empties us of our certainty and helps us accept our powerlessness. We claim our powerlessness, so God can be the power in us, the power that can do more than we can ask or imagine. The power to do the unimaginable.

I know how difficult all of this is, especially now. Who out there wants to empty themselves of what they know for certain is true? I will not ask for a show of hands.

But the truth is, amid all the talk about national unity, we are exactly where we were when that gym incident I described happened. We are not better than we were several years ago. In fact, things are worse, and we have moved from having gym fights to now having street fights and attempting to overtake the U.S. Capitol.

The same Rev. William Barber, when speaking at the inaugural prayer service for President Joe Biden, said, "We are in a jam today. Trouble is real, and whether we like it or not, we are in this mess together as a nation." Then, recalling the prophet Isaiah and the word he received from God,

Rev. Barber continued by saying,

> When this word of the Lord came to the prophet, his people were also in a jam. Bad leadership, greed and injustice and lies had led them into trouble, exile and economic hardship. . . . God said to the prophet, sound the trumpet. Tell the nation of its sin . . . tell the nation to repent of what got them here and turn in a new direction.[1]

The Scriptures reaffirm our need to take a look at our lives, as individuals and as a country, to come to terms with our sin and discover again how we can become a healing presence in the midst of conflict and injustice. Again and again, the Scriptures invite us to go into the desert of our hearts and with the psalmist, pray, "For God alone my soul in silence waits; from Him comes my salvation. He's solid rock under my feet and a breathing room for my soul" (Psalm 62:1–2, *Book of Common Prayer*). We are to go there and to ask Christ to help us see our lives and our world through his eyes, so that we may see what is not yet aligned with his will. We are to fast and pray and sit in expectancy, allowing God to catch us, just like a fisherman would catch fish. To catch and save us from the world of our own making and transport us into a world where his love and peace can be our very heartbeat.

But God's love is not just about playing nice and his peace is not without tensions. The Hebrew word *shalom,* or "peace," is not just the absence of tension; it is the presence of justice. Unity that is not capable of naming social wrongs does not mean much, and a community that does not have a place for confession, repentance, and forgiveness is simply a time bomb waiting to explode. It is what psychologist M. Scott Peck called a pseudo-unity or a pseudo-community, and it describes a group of people who "wanting to be loving, withhold some of the truth about themselves and their feelings in order to avoid conflict."[2] In that configuration, their differences and individual grievances are minimized and unacknowledged. They may appear to be functioning smoothly, but love and justice can never thrive in a pseudo-community.

Christians, in this crucial time, are called to something different—something that is bigger than a Republican or a Democratic ideal, that reflects Christ's transforming care and can enable us not to just play nice with one another but also address our difficulties, discern how we have participated in and, at times, caused other people's suffering, ask for forgiveness, and figure out a way to move into unity that also has room for accountability. We are called to move beyond politics as we know it, but not to forget about the political. Our political, however, has to go deeper than the surface analysis that is often easily available, to touch the heart of our real human needs. Our political needs to start with our stories.

And the stories we tell can be tools for justice when they are framed in their historical context, not shying away from hard truths, what the Poor People's Campaign has identified as systemic racism, poverty, the war economy, ecological devastation, and the nation's distorted moral narrative

of religious nationalism. While painful, this kind of historical reckoning is necessary. Not to bring shame, but to allow
the truth to free us. As the martyr Fr. Ignacio Ellacuría
reminds us, among the signs to guide us is "the one out-
standing present in every age, in whose light all the others
must be discarded and interpreted. That sign is always the
historically crucified people."[3]

We should start by walking through the chapters of our
country's history and seeing our stories in that context.
Stories of what helped or harmed the community. Stories of
injustices we've experienced, stories of injustices we have
caused or consented to, and moments of salvation we have
felt. It is then that we will be able to see beyond the limiting
options we're given. It is then that we will be able to fish for
one another's best selves. It is then that we will be able to
unite the poor and dispossessed across color lines and all
of the lines of division to build a mass social movement to
help each other enter what Dr. King called the beloved community. It is then that we will experience unity. Unity that
is not separate from justice.

Reverend Barber leaves us with the following questions
to reflect on:

Can America survive? Can America survive with over
87 million people uninsured or underinsured? Can
America survive with these fundamental attacks on
democracy? America is already to some degree an oli-
garchy. Decisions are being made by money in politics
rather than the votes of people. We are about to burst,

and we are bursting. Now the question is, where's the energy going to go? Because it's going somewhere. And it is always when a nation is about to burst that moral movements are birthed. If you do not have the moral movements, then that energy can go in directions that are utterly destructive. But that bursting can also be a birthing. As has been explained to me, when a woman has a baby, it is the most critical time between life and death, and the most creative time. Is this moment in America going to be a tomb or a womb? Is it going to be the burying of democracy, or is it going to be the birthing of a new freedom?[4]

On Being a Contemplative
in the World

People often ask me about contemplative life and whether it is possible to be a contemplative in the world in the context of one's responsibilities and struggles, loves and commitments. It was Father Bede Griffiths, an English Benedictine monk, who spent much of his life living in India in a Hindu-Christian ashram, who coined the phrase "universal call to contemplation." This phrase captures what was Fr. Bede's teaching, namely, that intimacy with God does not belong to a special group of religious professionals but is and should be available to all. It is our birthright. It is why we were born. It is why we are here, to open ourselves "to the inner mystery of the heart of reality" which is "the heart of each one of us."[1] To open ourselves to that love, to see the world through its eyes and to live from it with courage and commitment.

Commenting on this kind of life and how one gets there, Madeleine Delbrel, a French woman who spent most of her life working among the poor from a place of deep prayer, said the following:

There are some people God calls and sets apart in convents and monasteries. There are others God calls and leaves in society, the ones God does not "withdraw from the world." These are the people who have an ordinary job, an ordinary marriage or an ordinary celibacy. The people who have ordinary sicknesses and ordinary sorrows. The people who live in ordinary houses and wear ordinary clothes. These are the people of ordinary life. The people we meet on any ordinary street.

We believe that we lack nothing necessary here in the streets; if we did need something more, God would have already given it to us.

We, the ordinary people of the streets, have the distinct impression that solitude is not the absence of the world, but the presence of God.

For us, the whole world is the meeting place with the One whom we cannot avoid. We encounter God's living plan right there on the busy street corners. We encounter God's splendor in the laws of nature and science. We encounter God's imprint on the earth. We encounter Christ in all these "little ones" who are his own, the ones who suffer in their bodies, the ones who are bored, the ones who are troubled, the ones who are in need of something. We encounter Christ rejected in countless acts of selfishness.

Because we find that love is work enough for us, we don't take the time to categorize what we are doing as either "contemplation" or "action."

We find that prayer is action and that action is prayer. It seems to us that truly loving action is filled with light. It seems to us that a soul standing before such action is like a night that is full of expectation for the coming dawn. And when the light breaks, when God's will is clearly understood, she lives it out gently, with poise, peacefully watching her God inspiring her and at work within her. It seems to us that action is also an imploring prayer.

Godly solitude is the love of people, it is Christ serving Christ, Christ in the one who is serving and Christ in the one being served. How could such activity be for us a distraction from God or mere busyness and noise?

All this is the meeting place of God, minute by minute, the very place where God's love is revealed.[2]

To me, this captures beautifully what it means to be an engaged person of prayer in the world. It captures beautifully what we often call "new monasticism," a path that helps us live our lives by way of listening and responding to God in our midst.

When I speak of new monasticism I speak of a very broad impulse and movement that is felt and is emerging all over the world—communities that share in this mission and yet who don't necessarily belong to the same religious tradition. When I think of new monasticism I think of the Anglican new monastics in the United Kingdom with their many communities rooted in the Benedictine, Franciscan, and Ignatian spiritualities. I think of Sufi communities in Africa connected to a holy Sufi saint Sheikh Amadu Bàmbain in Senegal, who committed to nonviolent resistance against French colonial oppression, and in the process established a movement that is still very strong today. I think of Zen master Thich Nhat Hanh's Order of Interbeing, which is a true example of Engaged Buddhism and whose teachings remind us that the kingdom of God is available to us here and now. And, finally, I think of the community that I belong to, the Community of the Incarnation, which practices and teaches an engaged contemplative spirituality that helps us to live our prayer lives in the context of listening and responding to the cry of the poor and the cry of the earth.

All this presents to us a fresh, multi-religious potential for a new way of being human and contributes to a future that can help us build a more just and compassionate tomorrow amidst the ruins of a world that has lost its way.

But all of this has to start with each of us. It has to start with my commitment to a practice of prayer. All of this has to start with my adopting a way of life that can help me grow and nourish my spiritual life, including building community, so that I may become God's hands and feet and microphone for healing and justice. So here are a few parting words of advice on how to get going in this direction. Start with one or two suggestions on this list and then move to other suggestions as you are able. This process requires self-compassion and is meant to unfold one step and one day at a time.

- Protect yourself from a life of constant distraction and adopt a simple and modified life of digital minimalism, where you make conscious decisions about when the world can get hold of you and when you are unreachable and undistracted in your inner sanctuary of the heart (for instance, turning off your devices at a certain time each day or having a twenty-four-hour digital sabbatical in which you do not engage with electronics).

- Commit to a daily practice of contemplative prayer by spending thirty minutes in the morning and thirty minutes before sleep in a practice of talking to God, the kind of talking that leads to deep listening and receptive silence, a silence that speaks and loves. Make sure that at least some of your praying happens outside, in the natural world, with the earth. Practices like walking meditation, art as meditation, and mindful movement can also support your prayer. This will help you to discover your unique calling and how God wants to live, love and (maybe even protest) through you in the world.

- Practice the remembrance of God throughout the day, even in simple tasks. This may simply include an ongoing remembrance that "there is no place and no time outside of the present moment for an encounter with God"[3] and that to come home to God is to realize that, wherever you are, God is around you and within you.

- End the day with an examen asking God to help you see your day through Christ's eyes and reflecting on these four questions:

What am I grateful for today?

Where have I felt God's presence?

Where have I missed an opportunity to welcome God's presence or be Christ for others?

Is there anything I am sorry for?

Conclude with a prayer asking God for what you need for the next day to do better.

- Spirituality is a group activity, so look for a spiritual director who can guide you on your path. Eventually, every contemplative should also work with a therapist to avoid what psychologists call spiritual by-pass and be connected to a community where they can learn to practice vulnerability, confess their shortcomings, and learn how to ask for and receive forgiveness. Making this journey with a community of love and accountability is one of the greatest gifts of this path. After all, even Jesus had some good spiritual friends!

- Remember that all this is not for the sake of some kind of extraordinary mystical experience that can take you out of this world, out of your suffering, but rather, so that you can experience God, be changed by that experience, and then be sent into the midst of human suffering to be God's partner in transfiguring the world. This is for love and justice.

- Finally, love and justice are very specific; and justice, as Cornel West often reminds us, is really what love looks like in public. So to be loving,

- First commit to engaging with the world from a place of prayer, and not ideology; this gives you a felt sense of interconnectedness of all life in God and prevents othering.
- Second, commit to doing the work of coming to terms with your social location and how it relates to systemic racism, poverty, militarism, ecological devastation, and some of the distorted moral narratives that are so prevalent. Are there privileges you need to acknowledge or let go of? Are there commitments you need to reevaluate?
- Third, remember that talking about justice is not the same as doing justice, so simplify your life and commit to ethical living by buying all of your necessities in socially responsible, ecologically minded, and human-scale companies. As Arundhati Roy says, "The corporate revolution will collapse if we refuse to buy what they are selling."
- Practice works of mercy, making sure that your hands are touching the hands of someone who is suffering; include Mother Earth in that as well.
- Join a social movement, because changing your spending habits or serving others is only part of what is needed. Our lives and relationships do not happen in a vacuum but rather within institutions and systems that have their own crooked logic and are in need of massive changes.

As you do this, as you move toward a life of personal and political holiness, may your journey be blessed and may your life and presence remind those around you of God's presence. Deepening your connection to God, in you and around you, do not be afraid to feel the love, the joy, and also the pain that are present. Don't be afraid to have a heart and to risk breaking your heart. Feel into it all and know that every time you are touching the pain, you are touching the sacred wound of God. God who is always accompanying us and guiding us. God who is suffering with us. God who is moving us toward healing and liberation. God whose life-giving love and justice will one day be "all in all."

Appendix of Spiritual Practices

1. DAILY PRACTICE OF CONTEMPLATIVE PRAYER

I introduced this practice in chap. 3, and I consider this to be a foundational practice. I offer it here so you may easily practice it as often as you wish.

Before you begin this practice, recall St. Teresa's teaching on prayer. She said that prayer does not need to be difficult or complicated. Prayer is as simple as developing human friendships. She defined prayer as "an intimate sharing between friends." So imagine that you are about to spend some time with Someone you know loves you.

- At the beginning, sit down, take a few moments to center yourself by taking a couple of slow deep breaths, and then place yourself in the presence of Christ. You can literally imagine Christ sitting in front of you, remembering that he promised his friends that he will be with us always.
- Look at his face and see what you notice.
- Can you sense his love for you?
- Are you open enough to receive the gift of his love?
- Spend a few moments recognizing what is alive in you.
- When you are ready, tell him about what you are feeling

right now. Focus especially on your worries, your hurts, your problems as well as your joys and your triumphs. Take off your mask and really let your whole essence speak to God like that. If you do, some days there may be a lot of tears, and that can be a good thing.

- And when you're done telling Christ what is on your heart, when there are no more words to be said, just silently rest in his presence, letting him hold you.
- Do all of this for about twenty-five minutes.
- When you find yourself drifting away or losing your sense of Christ's presence, you can return to his presence again by recalling Christ sitting in front of you and saying, "Here I am, opening myself to you. Here I am, receiving you. Here I am, trusting you." This will help bring you back to a state of openness and receptivity. This will help you to rest in his love in a state of consent so he can do the work of healing on you.
- When your time is up, return to your breath, thank God for this time of quiet, and finish with a simple prayer of gratitude. I sometimes like to finish with the Prayer of St. Francis.

You can also combine this practice with a daily reading of the Gospel. After talking to God about what is present in your life and after naming some of the struggles and also joys, you ask God for a word of inspiration and direction, like ancient desert Christians did before approaching an elder. Then read the Scripture passage assigned for a day in a lectionary, and spend the next twenty-five minutes reflecting, talking, and listening to what God is saying to you about your life. Whenever you experience a sense of God's presence just simply rest, trusting in God.

2. OUTDOOR WALKING/MOVING MEDITATION

This practice is inspired by the Buddhist Zen master Thich Nhat Hanh and the Plum Village community. In their practice centers all over the globe, the community walks together slowly and silently outdoors every day for an hour through the forest or gardens, stopping to take in the natural beauty from time and time and also at times sitting down on the earth in receptive silence for a few minutes.

You can practice walking meditation in many different settings, outside or inside. It is essentially the practice of bringing our awareness to each step we are making. Every step helps us to fully arrive wherever we are, helping us see that there is no place and no time outside of the present moment for an encounter with God. As Thich Nhat Hanh teaches, we can walk in such a way that we kiss the earth with each step, expressing our reverence and kindness to ourselves and everything around us.

Adaptations
This practice can be adapted to moving mindfully for those of us in assistive devices. Bring all of your attention to your body moving through space as you feel your breath. You can also do this sitting down outdoors in nature. It is a form of prayer with the sacred earth.

- Begin by walking slowly and taking in everything that is present around you.
- Bring awareness to your breath, and notice each step that you take while you breathe in, and then each step you take while you breathe out.
- Breathing in, recite inwardly, "I am here," and breathing out, "I smile."
- Then start noticing what is around you—the fresh air, beautiful trees, the sun, birds, the presence of your beloved, etc., and continue to practice by including each of the things you notice in your meditation.
- "Breathing in, the fresh air is here; breathing out, I smile."
- "Breathing in, the beautiful trees are here; breathing out, I smile."
- "Breathing in, the sky is here; breathing out, I smile."
- "Breathing in, the birds are here; breathing out, I smile."
- You can repeat this phrase with anything else that you notice inspires you.
- Then move on to: "Breathing in, Mother Earth is here, giving us life and supporting us; breathing out, I smile."
- "Breathing in, God is here; breathing out, I smile."
- "Breathing in, my life with God is here; breathing out, I smile."
- "Breathing in, I take in all the gifts that this present moment brings me; breathing out, I say, 'Thank you.'"
- Take a few breaths in silence, and if you wish, begin again with the phrases, acknowledging everything that you are witnessing and connecting the awareness of it to

your breath and body. See how all of it is soaked with God's presence. See how you are really here, God is really here, and your life with God is really here in this present moment.

3. NIGHTLY EXAMEN

Father James Martin tells us

St. Ignatius Loyola used to say there was one prayer that his brother Jesuits should never miss praying daily . . . the examination of conscience [or examen] . . . Because . . . a prayerful review of the day, helps us to see where God is at work in our lives. And Ignatius knew that when we stop noticing this we start to feel distant from God. Moreover, since God communicates with us in our daily lives, we need to pay attention to what God is saying.[1]

So this simple practice can help us to "find God in all things" and "to take a magnifying glass to the seemingly ordinary, seeking to encounter the Divine."[2]

Here is a contemporary version of examen that I like to pray:

At the end the day, place yourself in the presence of God and ask God to help you see your day through Christ's eyes. Then reflect on the following five questions.

1. What comes to my mind and heart that you are grateful for today?

2. Ask the light of God's Spirit to guide you in reflecting on this day, on all that is moved within you and around you, and to see where God has been at work. Where were you most aware of God today? When did you feel most alive, most connected to God?

3. When were you least aware of God's presence? When did you feel least connected to God or lose sight of God?

4. Is there anything you regret from today? If so, bring it to God now.

5. Is there anything you would like to ask God's help or guidance with for tomorrow? Then place tomorrow in God's loving hands.

Conclude your meditation with the Lord's Prayer.

4. Saint Ignatius of Loyola's "Deathbed Exercise"

This meditative exercise was introduced early in the book, but it is so important that I would like to offer it here, for your easy reference and use.

- We are invited to imagine ourselves at the end of our lives, on our deathbed, or after our death facing Christ and reflecting in his presence and light on the regrets we have about our lives.
- So be in that imaginative place and allow yourself to see your life in that way.
- Take as much time as you need; and at least three to five minutes.

- From that imaginative place, ask yourself . . .
  - What kind of person have I been?
  - What kind of person have I failed to become?
  - What was the task that God brought me here to do?
  - What kind of thing was I born to fix in this world?
  - And, have I done that?

- Listen for God's answers, which will come with a sense of clarity of vision.
- Saint Ignatius then recommends that we ask God for signs to reassure us that we indeed are on the right path. One of the surest signs is a sense of internal peace—that feeling of rightness that we sometimes experience when we make the right decision.

5. CATHERINE DOHERTY'S *POUSTINIA* PRAYER PRACTICE

This practice, too, introduced in chap. 7, is offered here so that you will be able to access it easily and regularly.

Poustinia is Russian for "desert." The practice of *poustinia* calls us to dedicate time, perhaps a day a month, or a weekend a month, to solitude, prayer, and fasting. Here's how you do it:

- Go into a hermitage—this may simply be a room in your home or a place in nature—to be with God in silence.
- In this desert, you are freed from distractions.
- Try to fast only on bread and water while you are there.

- Bring only a Bible, and consult it, expecting that Jesus will use familiar words to offer you fresh wisdom.
- Open your heart to God. Bring to God everything that is weighing you down. Voice your problems, hopes, questions.
- Talk and then listen. Much of the time, nothing may happen. But if you stay with it, something will open up and guidance will come. You will "receive a word" from God that is directed to you. A word in the form of an intuition, or a scripture passage, or a feeling.

Notes

INTRODUCTION

1. "Loneliness and Community: An Interview with Henri Nouwen" (Mar.-Aug. 1994), Wineskins Archive, February 21, 2014, https://archives.wineskins.org/article/loneliness-and-community-an-interview-with-henri-nouwen-mar-aug-1994.

CHAPTER 1

1. Howard Thurman, *Meditations of the Heart* (Boston: Beacon Press, 1953), 15.

2. For a more detailed discussion of Genesis 1, see Shai Held, *The Heart of Torah, Volume 1. Essays on the Weekly Torah Portion: Genesis and Exodus* (Philadelphia: Jewish Publication Society, 2017), 7–12.

3. James H. Cone, *A Black Theology of Liberation: Fortieth Anniversary Edition* (Maryknoll, NY: Orbis Books, 2010), 99.

CHAPTER 2

1. Different versions of this story have been told by retreat leaders, pastors, and priests. Most likely this story was originally told by Brennan Manning (see https://www.youtube.com/watch?v=L5f2QqcRUmQ or Jared Story Blog at http://www.jaredstory.com/empty_chair.html).

2. Mirabai Starr, *Teresa of Avila: The Book of My Life* (Boston: New Seeds, 2008), 53.

CHAPTER 3

1. James Martin, SJ, "To Be a Saint, Just Be Who You Are," *America* magazine, Febrtuary 8, 2019, https://www.america magazine.org.

CHAPTER 4

1. To learn more about Bear Heart see his book, *The Wind Is My Mother: The Life and Teachings of a Native American Shaman* (New York: Berkley Books, 1998).

2. This interpretation of this passage is inspired by Bishop Robert Barron's commentary on this passage in one of his talks.

CHAPTER 5

1. Matthew Fox, "Advent: 2020," Daily Meditations with Matthew Fox, reflection for December 5, 2020, https://daily meditationswithmatthewfox.org.

CHAPTER 6

1. Anthony de Mello, "The Mystic Rickshaw Driver," DeMello Spirituality Center, https://www.demellospirituality.com.

2. Anthony de Mello, "Spirituality Means Waking Up," DeMello Spirituality Center. https://www.demellospirituality.com.

3. Frank Ostaseski, *The Five Invitations: Discovering What Death Can Teach Us about Living Fully* (New York: Flatiron Books, 2017), 1.

4. As quoted in Frank Ostaseski, *The Five Invitations*, 3.

5. Brian J. Pierce, *We Walk the Path Together: Learning from Thich Nhat Hanh and Meister Eckhart* (Maryknoll, NY: Orbis Books, 2005), 29.

CHAPTER 7

1. As quoted in Kaira Jewel Lingo, *We Were Made for These Times: Ten Lessons on Moving through Change, Loss, and Disruption* (Berkeley, CA: Parallax Press, 2021), ix.

2. Thich Nhat Hanh, *Living Buddha, Living Christ: 20th Anniversary Edition* (New York: Penguin, 2007), 30–31.

3. Omer Tanghe, *As I Have Loved You: Catherine de Hueck Doherty and Her Spiritual Family* (Dublin: Veritas Publications, 1988), 23.

CHAPTER 8

1. See John Shea, *The Spiritual Wisdom of the Gospels for Christian Preachers and Teachers* (Collegeville, MN: Liturgical Press, 2010), 269.

CHAPTER 9

1. Thomas Moore, "A Dark Night of the Soul and the Discovery of Meaning," January 4, 2021, *Kosmos Journal*, https://www.kosmosjournal.org.

2. See Mirabai Starr's introduction in her translation of St. John of the Cross' *Dark Night of the Soul* (New York: Riverhead Books, 2003), 11.

3. Martin Luther King Jr., *Stride toward Freedom: The Montgomery Story* (New York: Harper & Row, 1958), 114–15.

4. Richard Tarnas, "Is the Modern Psyche Undergoing a Rite of Passage?," *ReVision* 24, no. 3 (winter 2002): 2, *OneFile*, link.gale.com/apps/doc/A86429835/AONE?u=nysl_oweb&sid=google Scholar&xid=ee3d926e.

5. Johann Wolfgang von Goethe, as quoted in Kingsley L. Dennis, *New Revolutions for a Small Planet: How the Global Shift in Humanity and Nature Will Transform Our Minds and Lives* (London: Watkins Publishing, 2012), extract to open chap. 3.

6. Matthew Fox, *Julian of Norwich: Wisdom in a Time of Pandemic and Beyond* (iUniverse, 2020), 46–47.

CHAPTER 10

1. J. Hemmings, "The Brave Catholic Priest Who Volunteered to Die in a Stranger's Place," War History Online, August 1, 2020, https://www.warhistoryonline.com. For a more extensive review of Kolbe's life, see Elaine Stone, *Maximilian Kolbe* (New York: Paulist Press, 1997).

2. Betty Lifton, *The King of Children: The Life and Death of Janusz Korczak* (New York: Macmillan, 1997).

3. This formulation is inspired by Bishop Robert Barron's Holy Thursday sermon from April 9, 2020, https://www.youtube.com/watch?v=HzMr-Hb8jB8.

4. Ronald Rolheiser, *Sacred Fire: A Vision for a Deeper Christian and Human Maturity* (New York: Image Books, 2017), 231.

5. Ronald Rolheiser, *Our One Great Act of Fidelity: Waiting for Christ in the Eucharist* (New York: Image, 2015), 67.

CHAPTER 11

1. Sarah Coakley, lecture at Salisbury Cathedral, "Meaning beyond Meaning: Meditations on the Death and Resurrection of Jesus," March 30, 2013, https://www.abc.net.au.

2. Ronald Rolheiser, "Jesus, the Passion, and the Garden of Gethsemane," an excerpt from *The Passion and the Cross* (Cincinatti: Franciscan Media, 2015), https://www.franciscanmedia.org.

3. John of the Cross, *Dark Night,* Book 2:10, 1. (I have combined translations of Mirabai Starr, Kieran Kavanaugh, OCD, and Otilio Rodriguez, OCD.)

4. Inspired by Dorothee Sölle's (1929–2003) poem, "Dream me, God."

CHAPTER 12

1. Paul VI, Insegnamenti, VI, 377; P. J. Rosato, "Cena del Signore e amore sociale," 83, as quoted in "Sign of the Sacred: The Poor as Sacrament," Network FAMVIN, https://famvin.org/en/files/2016/12/poor-as-sacrament.pdf.

2. Gustavo Gutiérrez, OP, as quoted in "Sign of the Sacred: The Poor as Sacrament," https://famvin.org/en/files/2016/12/poor-as-sacrament.pdf.

CHAPTER 13

1. Derek Walcott, "Derek Walcott 1992 Nobel Lecture," NobelPrize.org, https://www.nobelprize.org.

2. Matthew Fox, "Entering into the Ground of Being," Daily Meditations with Matthew Fox, June 9, 2021, https://dailymeditationswithmatthewfox.org.

3. Matthew Fox, *Original Blessing: A Primer in Creation Spirituality Presented in Four Paths, Twenty-Six Themes, and Two Questions* (New York: Tarcher/Putnam, 2000), 37.

4. Gerhard von Rad, quoted in Brevard S. Childs, *Biblical Theology of the Old and New Testaments: Theological Reflection on the Christian Bible* (Minneapolis: Fortress Press, 2011), 102.

CHAPTER 14

1. Daisy Grewal, "How Wealth Reduces Compassion," *Scien-*

tific American, April 10, 2012, https://www.scientificamerican.
com.

CHAPTER 15

1. Henri J. M. Nouwen, *Bread for the Journey: A Daybook of Wisdom and Faith* (New York: HarperOne, 2006), January 26.

2. To read about the story of Jean Claude's healing and forgiveness, see Jean Claude, "After Genocide: An Astonishing Story of Forgiveness and Redemption," https://compassionrwanda.com.

CHAPTER 16

1. Translation by Bruce Chilton in *Rabbi Jesus: An Intimate Biography* (New York: Crown Publishing, 2002), 181.

2. This interpretation was inspired by Ronald Rolheiser's discussion of this passage in *Sacred Fire*, 109.

CHAPTER 17

1. Based on Karl Rahner, quoted in Rolheiser, *Sacred Fire*, 250.

2. Ronald Rolheiser, "In Exile," November 13, 2014, *Mississippi Catholic*, https://www.mississippicatholic.com.

3. Symeon the New Theologian, "Hymn 15," from his collected *Hymns of Divine Love* (various editions); also Galatians 2:20.

CHAPTER 19

1. Reverend Barber's sermon, delivered at Washington National Cathedral on January 21, 2021, and is available online in many places, including *Time* magazine's website, https://time.com.

2. Meryn G. Callander, "Four Stages of Community" (n.d.), adapted by Callander from M. Scott Peck, *The Different Drum: Community Making and Peace* (New York: Touchstone, 1998), https://atlc.org/members/resources/four_stages_community.html.

3. As quoted in Jon Sobrino, *No Salvation outside the Poor: Prophetic-Utopian Essays* (Maryknoll, NY: Orbis Books, 2008), 3.

4. To see complete interview with Rev. Barber go to: https://www.salon.com/2021/09/20/rev-william-j-barber-ii-america-is-now-at-the-most-critical-time-between-life-and-death.

AFTERWORD

1. See the important book on these teachings of Fr. Bede Griffiths by Cyprian Consiglio, *Prayer in the Cave of the Heart: The Universal Call of Contemplation* (Collegeville, MN: Liturgical Press, 2010).

2. Madeleine Delbrel, *We, the Ordinary People of the Streets,* trans. David Louis Schindler Jr. and Charles F. Mann (Grand Rapids, MI: Eerdmans, 2000), 54–58.

3. Brian J. Pierce, *We Walk the Path Together*, 29.

APPENDIX

1. James Martin, SJ, *In All Seasons, For All Reasons: Praying throughout the Year* (Collegeville, MN: Liturgical Press, 2017), 19.

2. "The Ignatian Examen," September 24, 2020, Midwest Province, https://www.jesuitsmidwest.org.

Acknowledgments

Some people write their books in isolation, but for me writing is a profoundly communal practice. What I write is often initially seeded by the spoken word. The ideas in this book, for instance, first emerged from various talks, sermons, interviews, and conversations I shared with different groups. These many communities not only gave me an opportunity to teach, travel, and articulate my understanding of socially engaged contemplation, they also served as conversation partners, providing further clarification and helpful critique for the ideas presented here. I am especially grateful to Schumacher College (UK), St. Ethelburga Center for Peace and Reconciliation (UK), the interfaith community of contemplatives at the Contemplative Alliance, and the Global Peace Initiative of Women. I am also appreciative of the UK contingent of new monastics, especially Rev. Ian Mosby, for the support and friendship. Also, gratitude to The Rev. Hugh M. Grant and Rev. David McCallum, SJ, for their spiritual support. Finally, I am thankful for my colleagues at the Cathedral of the Incarnation, The Center for Spiritual Imagination, and the Community of the Incarnation, where much of what's in this book has been delivered in sermons. It is a true gift to be able to travel together and to learn from Dean Michael Sniffen, Mother Morgan Mercer Ladd, Kris Viera, Fr. John Merz, Fr. Michael Delaney, Fr. Eddie Alleyne, Deacon Denise Galloway, Fr. Bruce Griffith, Larry Tremsky, Kate Akerman, Charles Janoff, Gerry Potter, and Bishop Laurence Provenzano. Your wisdom and mentorship have deeply impacted my life.

This book would not have happened without the guidance of Jon Sweeney, a consummate writer and editor and my dear friend, who initially proposed that I write it. My gratitude also goes to those who provided a keen editorial eye which greatly improved early versions of these reflections: My friend and trusted collaborator Vania Kent, who helped develop new monastic spirituality working alongside me in the new monastic movement, and Dr. Katherine Wilson and her husband Fernando Reyero Noya, who also supported me through the process of writing and editing this book.

Finally, my deepest gratitude for Kaira Jewel, my beloved partner, who brings the wisdom of her many years as a monastic in the community of Thich Nhat Hanh into our daily life. Her embodiment of wisdom, kindness, generosity, joy, and tenderness of heart help me to touch God in a more simple and direct way. My dear KJ . . . thank you for being such a loving, kind, and wise partner and for helping me to be a better version of myself. I love you.

I dedicate this book to my teachers and mentors who have guided me over the years:

- My parents, Halina and Richard Bucko, for showing me what real love looks like.
- Matthew Fox, for being the true elder in my life, and for his friendship, mentorship, and love.
- Andrew Harvey, for teaching me to follow my heartbreak and helping me to "serve the growing Christ."
- Rabbi Yehuda Fine aka Times Square Rabbi, for passing on to me the mysticism of the streets and helping me look for the sparks of light in the darkest of places.

- Marcellus Bear Heart William, for helping me see my calling.
- Tessa Bielecki, for turning Teresa of Ávila into a friend I can rely on (and for her earthy mysticism).
- Sr. Vandana Mataji, for welcoming me into her Himalayan hermitage and making the teachings of Hindu-Christian monastics alive in a new way.
- Swami Satchidananda, for giving me a model of contemplative living early on in my life.
- Shree Anandi Ma, for helping me taste the holy.
- Ton Baba, for showing me a punk rock version of engaged spirituality in the slums of Delhi.
- Dr. Rod Bush, for introducing me to the Black radical tradition and helping me befriend Malcom X as a spiritual guide.
- Sr. Michaela and Br. Francis, for continuing to protect the silence and inviting us to be renewed by its holy embrace.
- Fr. Thomas Keating, for his wisdom, generosity, and grandfatherly care.
- Rev. Leng Lim, for sharing that first Eucharistic meal with me.
- Taslim Tagore, for the many years of serving young people struggling with homelessness together at the Reciprocity Foundation.
- All the Reciprocity Kids, for helping me learn what prayer means.

About the Author

Fr. Adam Bucko has been a committed voice in the movement for the renewal of Christian Contemplative Spirituality and the growing New Monastic movement. He has taught engaged contemplative spirituality for two decades on three continents and co-authored two books: *Occupy Spirituality: A Radical Vision for a New Generation* and *The New Monasticism: An Interspiritual Manifesto for Contemplative Living*. He is widely known among new monastics, religious and social progressives, and by spiritual seekers across generations from millennials, through his work with young activists, to boomers, given his work with Matthew Fox, Thomas Keating, Tessa Bielecki, Richard Rohr, Mirabai Starr, and Andrew Harvey.

Committed to an integration of contemplation and just practice, he co-founded an award-winning non-profit, The Reciprocity Foundation, where he spent fifteen years working with homeless and LGBTQ youth living on the streets of New York City, providing spiritual care, developing programs to end youth homelessness, and articulating a vision for spiritual mentoring in a post-religious world. He currently serves as a director of The Center for Spiritual Imagination at the Episcopal Cathedral of the Incarnation in Garden City, NY, and is a member of The Community of the Incarnation, a dispersed new monastic community dedicated to democratizing the gifts of monastic spirituality and teaching contemplative spirituality in the context of hearing and responding to the cry of the poor and the cry of the earth.

He lives in New York with his partner, Kaira Jewel Lingo, a Buddhist teacher and former nun in the community of Thich Nhat Hanh. Together they lead The Buddhist-Christian Community for Meditation and Action. To learn more about his work go to www.adambucko.com.